# THE
# THOUGHT
# WAR

## Volume One

MARY BANKS

# TABLE OF CONTENTS

# INTRODUCTION

When I sat down to write this book, I became concerned and perplexed about writing a book that could only be understood from a born-again perspective. After thirty-five years of writing and ministering to those who confess a relationship with our Lord, how do I now write to include those who do not know Him, but are held captive by their emotions, desires, lusts, hurts and disappointments? How do I reach that wife who has to deal with a cheating husband and those off-the-chain children? Though some of us may have found our way to deliverance and the sweetness of freedom, there are so many who have not been as fortunate. But then our God is faithful to reach out to all of us with the great love He is so well known for.

Whether saint or sinner, we all have been given a conscience by our Creator. It is the conscience of man that knows God and the moral goodness we were intended to live by. Likewise, whether you are saved or not, evil is your enemy. It robs us of a happy, peaceful, fulfilling life. It is no respecter of persons, and it finds its way into the best of homes and hearts.

I have counseled hundreds of people who found themselves trapped inside circumstances, situations and relationships that caused frustration, depression, obsessions, bitterness, offenses and unforgiveness. But now more than ever, with our world seemingly collapsing all around us, there is a feeling of hopelessness that is beginning to overwhelm mankind. Many hearts are beginning to faint, just from listening to the daily newscasts. We are in a time of war and rumors of wars. Morality seems to be a thing of the past; loyalty has succumbed to betrayal and hope for the future is vanishing daily. The effect of these times on the world is being manifested in diverse emotions and cynical behavior.

Financial failures, political diversities, marital frustrations and the overall stress of our times are the woes of these days. But for the Christian, these represent fiery trials that come to try our faith. Nevertheless, both saved and unsaved have merged in character and ever-increasing fear and hopelessness. This book is purposed to bring attention to the distance we have fallen from righteousness and peace, as well as the fierce departure of man from his own conscience. Hopefully, it will also lead the way to the peace that can only be found in truth.

The question was raised in one of our meetings: "What words would your friends, family members, or co-workers use to describe you if they had to be totally honest?" In many cases words like *mean, hateful, contentious* and *unforgiving* might be used. In other cases, *depressing, bitter, controlling, jealous* and *offensive*, might be on the list.

Over the years, I learned that 99% of deliverance is identification. The other 1% is submission to the Word and will of God. It is not about what church we attend or what our social status is. It is about coming back to the purpose for which we were created. It is about walking

out of the snare of negative behavior and condemnation, to becoming whole and at peace with God and man.

Jesus said, "The truth will make you free." Well, it is time to examine our very own contributions to the ills of our heart and the wounds in our soul. Wrong thinking is the root of evil. The thoughts inside negative mindsets have become as a dagger, piercing the mantle of righteousness and skillfully cutting it away leaving no evidence of the life of Christ we confess or the goodness we desire to experience from others.

How will the world know that Jesus did come in the flesh if not by the righteous disposition of the Sons? The fleshy mind is the tool many use to walk through circumstances, situations and relationships. They reject or ignore the mind of Christ and proceed to handle things without the wisdom of God or the counsel of His Spirit.

But how does the scripture instruct those who testify in the Lord? Does it not warn us against walking in the vanity of our own mind? To do so, is to have the understanding darkened; and this darkness alienates us from the life of God and causes blindness of heart. Because sin is progressive, we are ushered into a state of spiritual numbness that the Word describes as being *past feeling and given over to lasciviousness and uncleanness with greediness (Ephesians 4:19).* But this is not Christ, nor is it what we have learned of Christ. We were taught to put off or destroy the former lifestyle of the old man.

When I began to teach ministers and others *"How to Walk in the Spirit,"* it created quite a controversy in the religious community. Of course, the contention was among those who call themselves leaders in the church world today. They raked me over the coals for even suggesting born-again believers in Christ could live a life free from sin and evil desires. And now I dare to suggest that they can live a life that trades anguish and anxiety for joy and peace. They can exchange despair for hope and a great expectation; hatred and iniquity for love and forgiveness.

Are these not the truths that are at the very core of the gospel of Jesus Christ? Or, are these just slogans found on tee-shirts and church billboards? Are we now to believe that after nearly two thousand years of survival this Gospel has no power in it? Is the Bible simply another compilation of philosophies that have no true meaning in the real world?

Furthermore, one would have to ask why there is such controversy over something that is clearly commanded in the scriptures, and even more, why is this controversy coming from those who preach and teach the scriptures. People, including Christians are hurting, afraid, emotionally distraught and living in despair. These are facts. But what about the abundant life ministers have been promising for as long as I can remember? Where is the peace of God that passes understanding? Where is the '*joy of the Lord*' that is supposed to be our strength? These questions deserve answers.

The pages of this book will go to the heart of these matters.

We will explore the truth about the life God intends for us to live, as well as discover just how and what it takes to live it. Our souls have been put in jeopardy by some of the erroneous teachings that have been offered to the Body of Christ and the world. Our minds and hearts have been shaped by the philosophies of men who have left us spiritually frail and afraid of the days ahead. Is this the Mind of Christ: to be fearful and afraid, full of anguish and anxiety, hopelessness and despair? I think not, and I suggest to you that the Mind of Christ is only a breath away. To get there however, you must first win "The Thought War."

*The Thought War* is a work given to me by God to bring the world and the church face to face with itself. It reveals the cunning operations of our mind and soul that lead us into degradation, despair, separation from one another and God. It not only offers the *why*, but also reveals the *how*. It tells us how we got in some of the mess and mindsets we find ourselves in. But more than that, it shows us the way out. It tells us why we hurt for so long, but then how to heal instantly.

Take the time to read this book or listen to the audio book. It will not only deliver, but also inspire you to bring that deliverance to your loved ones, friends and even strangers.

Be Blessed.

# TRAINED TO FAIL

As I began to write I suddenly realized that my mind was being bombarded by the approved book-writing protocol of our day. I found myself becoming nervous as to how I would present the message. But then I thought, I have written over two hundred study guides and books that have been changing lives at Bible Teachers Global Training Centers and Bible Teachers International Worship Centers for nearly three decades. Now that we are introducing this Word to the Church at large, it is the same Word, presented in the same fashion that will perfect the Body.

I want you to follow me as I take you on a journey to the eternal purpose of God: the spiritual perfection of His Sons. However, in order to make this trip, you must meet the criteria the Father has set before us. ***You must agree that the holy Word of God is the authority that will settle all controversy.*** You must also open your heart to receive truth that may in fact shatter your present belief system.

Before I came into the revelation of perfection through the life of Christ in me, (see my book, *"Be Ye Perfect"*), I believed even as most Christians; that the fleshy mind was my worst enemy. But then I read that it is with the mind that I serve the Lord (Romans 7:25). So then, if the mind is the mechanism by which I am to serve the Lord, why was it always the culprit in my failures? I am sure most of you have felt the same frustrations and sense of hopelessness.

1

I wanted to live a life pleasing to God. I wanted to walk in the power realm of the Spirit. I had such great hopes of spiritual accomplishments in ministry. I was to be like Paul, Peter and John. I would be one of those whose very shadow would heal the sick. What I became though was a born-again believer constantly missing the mark, crippled by emotions and depressed by life. However, I knew enough to know that this was not what the Father intended to be the life of a Son.

## St. John 7:38

*He that believeth on me, as the scripture hath said, out of his belly shall flow rivers of living water.*

We agreed to allow the Word to be the authority in this discussion. If you dare to accept the heart and mind of the Father in this matter you will begin to experience joy, peace and even righteousness. You will break the flesh barrier, passing through the veil to life in the Kingdom of God.

The living water Jesus speaks of here is the Holy Ghost (John 7:39). Jesus also said it is not that which goes into a man that defiles him, but that which comes forth out of him. The Lord implies that only those things pertaining to the Spirit of God will proceed from those who believe on Him according to the scriptures. Now this may seem very mundane to you, but I declare that this is the number one problem in the Church today. The saints do not believe on Christ the way the scriptures have presented Him. Now your mind may go to His Coming or His crucifixion or maybe His return and say, *"Oh, yes, I do believe."* But I do not speak here of those events; I speak of His sojourning in you. It is His indwelling in your flesh and what that has afforded you that are the issues here. It is of those things that I speak concerning your unbelief.

Nevertheless, I know of no other way to bring you to the place you seek in Him, except you believe as the Word has proclaimed. Acceptance of the Word at face value is the only weapon you have against the workings of your fleshy mind and the perversions of your soul. It is the Word that will make you free.

**Romans 12:1-2**
*1 I beseech you therefore, brethren, by the mercies of God, that ye present your bodies a living sacrifice, holy, acceptable unto God, which is your reasonable service.*
*2 And be not conformed to this world: but be ye transformed by the renewing of your mind, that ye may prove what is that good, and acceptable, and perfect, will of God.*

Paul, the messenger of the Lord Jesus Christ and apostle to the church, infers that the church at Rome can live in the presence of God and man without conforming to the way of the world. Now I am sure you have heard this principle taught many times before. However, what does it really mean? It implies that we are to be different in our ways and character. There are many other scriptures that support this belief; passages such as, *"...What fellowship has light with darkness," (2 Corinthians 6:14)* or, *"Love not the world, nor the things in the world," (I John 2:15)* or even *"Ye are a peculiar people" (I Peter 2:9).* Though these all refer to a creature totally oblivious to the ways and things of the world, this is certainly not true regarding the Sons of God today.

The Body of Christ is confused. The mind of the church has been consistently assailed by traditions, isms and schisms of men. In fact, there are many false doctrines that have systematically poisoned the people of God, the deadliest of which are *"Faith and Prosperity", "Dual Nature" and "The Doctrine of Grace(wherein there is no penalty for sin)"* doctrines. These doctrines and traditions have created mindsets that totally contradict the eternal purpose of God. They have fashioned a creature that is not even a facsimile of a real son of God.

According to Webster's Dictionary, a **mindset** is **a mental attitude or a fixed state of mind.** There has been much ado about mindsets in the preaching of the gospel. However, most of these discussions have done nothing more than confirm the great lie satan has perpetrated in the church: *"Nobody is perfect."* This mindset is the most horrid affront to the sacrifice of our Lord and Savior, Jesus Christ.

As we proceed to talk about living in the imagination, or deliverance from hurts, unforgiveness, frustration, desire, depression, obsession, jealousy or control, I realize that there is no such deliverance unless you hear and receive the truth about salvation. I guarantee that if you have your heart open to receive these truths, by the time these captivities are discussed here, you will be able to deliver yourself from any snare in which the mind has found itself entrapped.

First of all, the mind is not an evil thing in your body. Webster defines it as *(a) the element or complex of elements in an individual that feels, perceives, thinks, wills, and especially reasons; (b) the conscious mental events and capabilities in an organism; and (c) the organized conscious and unconscious adaptive mental activity of an organism.*

Remember, according to scripture, the mind is the mechanism by which you are to serve the Lord. So then, how did it become the enemy of the soul? I submit to you that it is through false doctrines and the ignorant teaching of salvation that this mental albatross has been created for the saints of God. I, too, was once guilty of teaching such ignorance. It was the grace and mercy of God that stopped me in my tracks and set my feet on the path of knowledge and wisdom that changed my life and my ministry forever.

The word I had received trained me to fail in God. It made me expect to miss the mark periodically. Oh, it was a stickler against fornication, adultery, drinking and other vices, but it never arrested the evil thoughts, negative character or painful emotions I suffered year after year. Its basic theme was, *"nobody is perfect."* Thus, it created a belief system that accepted occasional sin as a way of life. Before coming into the knowledge of the truth, I heard my daughter Tanya, say, *"There is no way this sinless Christ could relate to me in any place other than atonement."* His life and mine were totally separate in character and desire.

Furthermore, the prosperity message recreated in me a thirst for worldly success. I wanted the things of this world: money, notoriety, and the good life. But Christ said to take no thought for such things. I suppressed hurts and deep emotional pain in the name of bearing the infirmities of others. Paul insisted I press toward the mark of perfection, but the message declared perfection to be unobtainable for the saints of God. This drove me to a place where my mind nearly collapsed under the weight of wantonness, frustration, fear, pain, ignorance and confusion.

The first thing the Father did was to assure me that what I had been hearing and preaching as the gospel was indeed not His Word at all. It had elements of truth, but these truths were set in the wrong perspective, thus forging the great lie; a Son of God who is at times, emotionally and spiritually crippled. It was the grace of God that rescued me.

Secondarily, He took me out of tradition and set me on the path of the Spirit. I was systematically taught a progressive Word by Him that moved me and others to a place of righteousness, love, joy and peace in the Holy Ghost. We discovered we could live holy twenty-four hours a day, seven days a week. But more than that, we discovered liberty; the freedom from hurts and hopelessness associated with disappointments, frustration, depression and, yes, sin.

Thirdly, I received my commission: *"Even as I sent Moses into the land of Egypt to bring my people out of slavery, I am sending you to my Church to bring my people out of ignorance."* This was the word God the Father spoke, as

I lay prostrate on my bedroom floor. This is the reason I come to you now, with the first of many truths the Father has delivered unto me. I am sure that there are others, like myself, who have been hidden in His quiver these many years.

Be encouraged. The fact that the Father has allowed you to partake of these truths means He is mindful of you and desires to use you in His service.

# SONS OF GOD HAVE NO BIRTH DEFECTS

It is my responsibility as an apostle to the Body of Christ to identify and destroy any mindset that exalts itself above the knowledge of God. There are many teachings in the Body of Christ on the disposition of the mind that have grossly undermined the work of the cross. In this discussion the mind is used to refer to the soul or heart.

Let us take a look at the big picture for a moment. Depression, frustration, unforgiveness, jealousy, evil imagination etc., are all dispositions of the mind. They are mere manifestations of the operations that take place in the soul. Christianity has established spiritual psychiatric wards to deal with these ills. Thus, we have Christian Psychiatry designed to walk the Sons of God through their spiritual deficiencies. Our counseling appointments have become therapeutic sessions in which the clergy spends most of its time trying to heal or change mental dispositions.

This is heresy! Listen to me carefully. When we the leaders in the Body of Christ, entreat depression, unforgiveness, hurts from offenses, evil imaginations and such dispositions as birth defects in the children of God, we dishonor God and bring Christ to an open shame. I hope you will open your heart to hear what the Spirit is about to say to you.

Consider the following passages.

**James 3:10-12**
*10 Out of the same mouth proceedeth blessing and cursing. My brethren, these things ought not so to be.*
*11 Doth a fountain send forth at the same place sweet water and bitter?*
*12 Can the fig tree, my brethren, bear olive berries? either a vine, figs? so can no fountain both yield salt water and fresh.*

Look at the impossibilities here. A fig tree cannot produce olives, nor does a fountain send forth salt and fresh water. You must accept the principle here. If olives are found on a tree it is because the tree is an olive tree. If a fountain produces salt water, it is because the source of the fountain is salt water. The same is true of our walk in God.

God created each Son whole and complete, not emotionally crippled and wanton. If we walk after the flesh, we will mind the things of the flesh. Likewise, we will produce the character and emotions associated with the flesh. But if we walk after the Spirit, we will mind the things of the Spirit and produce the attributes and emotions of the Spirit of God. The bottom line is, it is impossible to walk after the Spirit and produce the character and emotions of the flesh.

Deep emotional pain, spiritual deficiencies, iniquity and wantonness are not attributes of the Spirit of God. In fact, there is no captivity of the mind that is characteristic of a born-again believer who walks after the

What is the mindset here? Leadership
accepted the great lie. They believe tl
always exist in the Body of Christ ar
always be defects in the born-again believer.

God is not impotent! He is mighty in all that He does.
Salvation is no exception. It is the mighty hand of God in
the salvation of the Sons that is on trial here. Every time
leaders in the Body entreat sin and emotional disorders
such as depression, frustration, offenses and unforgiveness
as spiritual deficiencies, they help to validate satan's
inference that God is an impotent God unable to keep that
which He saved out of the world. If the Sons of God were
born with birth defects that made them victims of the same
captivities as unbelievers, then where is the power of their
God?

I submit to you that it is the erroneous doctrines and
perspectives regarding the born again experience that is
at the root of this controversy. In all the years that I have
been a member of the Body of Christ, which are more
than fifty, I have never really heard the gospel of Jesus
Christ preached in its entirety. I have heard the message
of a suffering servant and redeemer. I have read many
books about the plight, the disposition and position of the
Sons even as you have. We have heard many preachers
proclaim the day of the manifested Sons of God. We
marched through the Christian theatrics and fads: *"Name
it and claim it," "The King's kids," "Step on the head of*

*vil,"* and the most hilarious of all, *"M o n e y ... teth."* We were even privileged to hear sermons exemplifying the fact that we can do all things through Christ.

But what was the bottom line? When the rubber met the road, we were still crippled by emotional pain, suppressing true desires and struggling to maintain righteous character on a daily basis. We went to conventions and conferences looking for the magic formula. We wanted to hear something that would end the struggle and cause us to walk in the power of the Holy Ghost. We knew enough to know that we were missing something. Because we didn't know what we lacked, we continued to hunger and search for the knowledge, the prophecy, or the laying on of hands that would finally catapult us into that long sought after place of power.

Most of us wanted to work ministry. So after long years of missing the mark and waiting for a *power miracle*, some left their seats of boredom and embarked on the trail of ministry that had been blazed by many who had the same frustrations. But I had never heard the truth about His indwelling in us until the Lord revealed this awesome reality to me.

Do you really believe that it is the heart and mind of God for His people to journey through life day after day trying to sort out their paths through a maze of false doctrines that promise the world but delivers nothing? What about inner healing counseling that can only place bandages on our wounds, and sermons, void of the power to perfect character? No wonder there is such hopelessness in the people of God. There has been so many years of false hope delivered to them, until the declaration that there are new voices with a new revelation coming to the forefront does very little to excite them. They have seen and heard too much. That is why the wisdom of God demanded that I remain at home with the flock until I produced the evidence of the truth I am sent to carry to the Body.

If I am not successful in making you understand this monumental principle, which is at the very core of your salvation, the writing of this book will have the same effect as putting a band-aid on a gunshot wound. You will have learned a few more truths without the power to execute them. THE KEY TO POWER IS THE KNOWLEDGE OF GOD. It is the sure Word, pure and full of the purpose of God. It is not doctrines devised from the failure of men to walk in the righteousness of God. I know that your struggle to live holy and to be free from lingering hurts can be over if I can make you know the truth about the things God has freely given to His children. Stop for a moment and pray that clarity will come to your heart as you embark on this journey to the heart and mind of the Father.

There are many who have grown up in the Lord with me and we are the proof that you can live in this world free from sin and the crippling emotions satan uses to snare the Sons. Continue to read and I will show you how to win *"The Thought War."*

# MIND & SOUL

When we think of the mind, we immediately think in terms of our brain. Often in general conversations we refer to our head as being 'full of thoughts' and cite it as the location of the mind. It is true that the brain is the control center for the body; it is the mind of the flesh. It is the place where knowledge is gathered through the five senses and stored in a place called memory. The brain's ability to process and reiterate that knowledge is called intellect. Because science never considers any explanation outside the physical, it concluded that we used only our brain (mind), to think and to reason.

However, the brain is a 'member' of the human body. It was a member of the human body before we were saved, and it is still a member of the body; just as an eye, ear or tongue. Though it is the control center for the body, it is still only a body part that is controlled by a greater power.

We cannot argue the fact that the brain is a place of thought. However, the fleshy mind (brain) can only give a physical interpretation of its environment. It is indeed the place where thoughts are assembled and formed into patterns and actions. But we can insert here that thoughts do not originate in the brain, they are simply assimilated there so that they can be expressed in words or deeds. The world calls this mental process, thinking. However, it might surprise us to see how God defines thought.

The scriptures are quite clear on this subject:

**Matthew 15:19**
> *For **out of the heart proceed evil thoughts,** murders, adulteries, fornications, thefts, false witness, blasphemies*

**Mark 7:21**
> *For from within, **out of the heart of men, proceed evil thoughts,** adulteries, fornications, murders*

**Luke 24:38**
> *And he said unto them, Why are ye troubled? And **why do thoughts arise in your hearts?***

**Matthew 9:4**
> *And Jesus knowing their thoughts said, Wherefore **think ye evil in your hearts**?*

These passages clearly reveal the fact that thinking begins in the heart; which is the capital of the soul. It is a spiritual exercise done by the inner man; which is also a term used to describe the soul. It is necessary to understand that these words, *"heart" "soul" "mind" "inner man," "spirit," "spirit of the mind"* and even on occasion, *"breath,"* are all used interchangeably in the scriptures.

The character of our thoughts is also determined in the soul or heart. The thoughts that proceed out of the heart are either good or evil. But where do they go? These thoughts are manifested in either conversations or deeds; if not, they are contained in the imagination. If our thoughts are revealed in conversation or deeds, they must be sent to the mind of the flesh, which is given permission to use its ability to express these thoughts in our spheres of influence.

The functions of the mind, namely its thought patterns, can be trained, influenced, and even manipulated. Scripture bears witness of this in its instructions to the church at Philippi. *Finally, brethren, whatsoever things are **true**, whatsoever things are **honest**, whatsoever things are **just**, whatsoever things are **pure**, whatsoever things are **lovely**, whatsoever things are of **good report**; if there be any **virtue**, and if there be any **praise**, think on these things (Philippians 4:8).* This passage sets the boundaries for our thinking. It is the parameters of thought given to the soul and passed on to the flesh.

These instructions were given to the soul. He is the originator of thought. It is the soul that is to ensure the fleshy mind remains within the boundaries of the faith. He is the power and master of the body. Though the fleshy mind is the control center for the workings of the flesh, the soul provides the mind with ***content, character*** and ***purpose***.

David understood that it is the heart (soul) that God holds responsible for the disposition of men and gave advice to his son accordingly.

## 1 Chronicles 28:9

*And thou, Solomon my son, know thou the God of thy father, and serve him with a perfect heart and* *with a willing mind: for **the Lord searcheth all hearts, and understandeth all <u>the imaginations of the thoughts</u>**: if thou seek him, he will be found of thee; but if thou forsake him, he will cast thee off for ever.*

Right here, I need to remind you again that the ***imagination*** is **a collection of thoughts that may or may not have been expressed. It is a holding place for our true disposition.** As you will learn later, it is an incubator for thoughts; with the sole purpose of keeping them alive and well. The imagination is a function of the soul or heart; therefore, ***the contents of the imagination serve also to provide spiritual location.*** Note that God searches the imagination for the good or evil of its thoughts. Thus, it is the content of the imagination that is truly what a man thinks. *For as he thinketh in his heart, so is he: Eat and drink, saith he to thee; but his heart is not with thee (Proverbs 23:7).*

Thoughts do not just pop up in our heads out of nowhere. They have an origin; and that origin is the soul. It is the desire of the soul that initiates thinking. The soul allows structures or rejects thoughts. The soul receives or rejects suggestions from satan or instructions from God.

In the beginning, man was made a living soul. You must understand that the body belongs to the soul. The soul is that eternal part of man that will live forever; either with God or in torment. The soul meditates on ways to accomplish its desires. The fleshy mind or brain is simply the member of the body the soul uses to bring those desires into reality.

For instance, the soul desires to feel the sensation of a cool breeze on its body. Therefore, it instructs the brain to send a message to the hands, which simply says, "Open the window." The point I seek to make here is that *the soul is the master of the body*.

The soul applies a spiritual interpretation to that which the body entertains or experiences. Science calls this a mental assessment, having no regard for the fact that all physical attributes have a spiritual origin. The body was merely a lump of clay before the spirit or soul was put into it. In other words, when a man touches a woman's hand, the brain or fleshy mind recognizes the sense of touch. However, the soul determines and dictates the connotation given to that touch. It decides whether it is benevolent or sensual.

Again, *the soul is the spirit of the mind*; it is the ruler of the house. It dictates or puts a definition on every experience. Its determinations supersede those of the fleshy mind or brain. A good example of this is *perversion*. The term means **an alteration of something from its original meaning, purpose or state, to something abnormal or corrupt and unacceptable. It is a distortion or corruption of what was originally intended.**

For instance, there are those who experience sexual acts that are degrading and even very painful to the human body. However, if the soul determines the pain to be pleasure, then that which the mind (brain) once processed as unnatural affection becomes perverted. The mind is forced to accept pain as pleasure. Once this operation is successful, then the fleshy mind now processes thoughts regarding sex differently, thus creating different emotions as well. From this point on, what the body sees, hears and feels, must conform to the criteria the soul has set.

**This type of perversion also establishes a mindset regarding sex**. The method by which any type of sexual thought or act is processed is set by the dictates of the spirit of the mind. Thus, painful degrading sex becomes a preference and may even be considered normal for that individual.

Again, man was made a living soul and it is the soul, not the body that will give an account of the deeds done in the flesh. The body is on its way back to the dust of the earth.

So then, what is the role of the mind? To answer this question, we must first set the proper perspectives. We must first define man or son of God from the Father's point of view. Remember, in the scriptures the words mind and soul are used interchangeably. However, in every instance the sons of God are instructed to bring their bodies under or put them in submission to the will and Spirit of God. This may seem to be a difficult thing to accomplish and it indeed would be, had we not been given the mind of Christ. The Holy Ghost is the indwelling of the Lord Jesus Christ. When we walk in the Spirit of Christ, we are simply walking in His mind, heart, and desires. This we will discuss in more detail in a later chapter.

Nevertheless, for now, it will suffice you to know that when the Lord speaks to us, He does not speak to the flesh; He speaks to the inner-man. He does not talk to the house; He talks to the master of the house. Therefore, the man, from God's perspective, is our inner man, who upon salvation was placed in the Holy Ghost; *for in Him we live and move and have our being.*

The Father has given instruction as to what the soul or heart is to focus its thoughts on: things that are honest, just, pure and lovely; things that are of good report, virtuous and praiseworthy. If our thoughts are structured according to God's design, they would produce a pattern of righteousness and godly character. To think outside of these boundaries is to devise evil and iniquity in the heart.

Before I end this chapter, I want to also clarify some terminology for the sake of going forward in our discussion. The fleshy mind or brain is the control center for the flesh; nevertheless, it is flesh. Therefore, when the term *mind* is used in scripture, it is sometimes referring to the human brain. In other instances, it is clearly referencing the soul. However, the soul gives life to the flesh including the mind (brain), which is also flesh. Therefore, it is the spiritual man that is held responsible for the deeds done in the body, including the thoughts of the heart and mind.

In conclusion, the mind of the flesh does not provide the nature of man, it simply responds to the influence of our nature. It is a place where man can process his environment and experiences. It is the knowledge and comprehension center of the flesh. The fleshy mind or brain is flesh, however, and spirit is always more powerful than flesh. It is the spirit of the mind (soul) that dictates how that which we entertain or interact with is processed. The soul has authority over the fleshy mind. Here is where likes and dislikes are born, affections are created and will is determined. The mind is always controlled, whether by the Spirit of God or by the soul of its master.

# THE MAKING OF A MINDSET

We have often heard it said, "We are the sum of our environment." If this is the case, then our mentality is shaped by experiences we encountered within these diverse environments.

## DIRECT EXPERIENCES

Direct experiences are circumstances, situations and relationships we actually lived through. Our very thought patterns are rooted and grounded in what we have seen, heard or felt.

In some instances, we might have been able to maintain a degree of control as to the disposition or outcome of these circumstances, situations and relationships. In others, that might not have been the case. In such instances, helplessness and fear factors would magnify the effect each of these circumstances, situations and relationships had on our personality.

## HARDSHIPS

I was born-again, but I woke up one morning and discovered that after many years of marriage, I was a single parent with three children to raise, no job and a non-financially rewarding career in evangelism. Oh, up to that point I had been strong in the Lord. I had never wavered in the midst of external temptations. I took pride in the fact that regardless of how hard things were, I would never betray God. My resolve was to wait on God who would surely bring about a change in my situation. After all, I was working for Him.

Well, a change did come. Things got worse and I got tired. I got tired of living on thirty and forty dollar offerings. When I did minister in a setting that was able to raise a three or four hundred-dollar love offering, my bills were so far behind that it didn't seem like very much at all. There was never enough to come out of the hole. First, the lights were turned off, then the water. We lit candles to eat by and dipped water out of the swimming pool in order to bathe. I needed to get a job or do something else. Preaching the gospel was not supplying the needs.

I was frustrated, depressed and heading into deep despair. All these were direct experiences that had a tremendous mental effect on my children and me. Regarding the knowledge of God and godliness, I was a babe in comparison to what I know now. Therefore, my responses to these experiences were also those of a babe. I knew nothing about purpose, son training or walking in the Spirit. I simply wanted relief from the situations of my life.

For those who are born-again, keep in mind that we are discussing the roots of behavior patterns that are the characteristics of the old man; (the man who did not know Christ). It is true; the born-again believer is a new creature, regenerated by the Spirit of God. Nevertheless, if

24

he should ever move off course, or rather walk outside the boundaries of the faith, he too, would walk in that which he remembers or once lusted after. He will return to the old ways of the old man.

## BETRAYAL

A friend of mine discovered her husband was cheating on her with one of her friends. She divorced him and vowed that she would never allow anyone else to get that close to her again. She actually lived through the horror of knowing her husband was having an affair. She lived through the drama of her best friend betraying their friendship. The experience left her bitter and never trusting anyone else. She is having severe problems in her second marriage due to a lack of trust and the unwillingness to become completely vulnerable to her present husband.

Without spiritual development and the knowledge of the truth, direct experiences can have a very negative effect on your perspective of life. Begin to think on those negative direct experiences you have lived through, and try to judge whether they have shaped your personality in a way that hinders you in relationships with God and/or man.

## INDIRECT EXPERIENCES

Indirect experiences can be characterized as exposure to or the witnessing of the experiences of others. This may be seen in our personal relationships, various forms of news media, and in one of the greatest influences on the mind today, television.

Little do we realize that everything our five senses entertain makes an impression on our soul. In the case of television, many are not aware of the deep messages engraved in the mind, even from childhood. These messages have formed mindsets, shaped the thought patterns and in many instances, the behavior of many adults today.

## FEARFUL AND UNBELIEVING

A young man listens to the news regarding a plane crash killing all 246 passengers. He vows never to get on a plane. He fears it so much until when an emergency arises that requires him to fly to the city in question, the trip becomes extremely stressful. Even if he experiences a perfect flight, he has a mindset about flying. He is unable to consider flying without anticipating a tragic accident.

The television news afforded him an indirect experience that has hindered his servitude to God and man to this day. His mindset about flying is grounded in fear. This he knows and understands. He is also aware of how it totally negates his testimony of trust in God. However, he has developed another mindset that circumvents that lack of trust, i.e., "I don't have to answer to or discuss my disposition with anyone, I am an adult. If I don't want to fly, I don't have to."

Every instruction of the Holy Spirit must also contend with that mindset. If God should have need of the young man in places that require flying to get there, then He too is an intruder seeking to invade his rights as an adult. The only hope to change this response is to go to the root of the problem. You see, our relationship with God must be one of trust, which includes loyalty to truth and obedience to His will. We cannot say that we are slaves to His will in one breath and usurp authority over that will in another. Nevertheless, such responses manifest our walk in the flesh.

The scriptures declare fear to be torment and it will continue to be torment until overcome. Perhaps one day the young man will come to the revelation of these truths, relinquish his rights to self guidance, and allow the Holy Spirit to lead him into a trusting relationship with God, as well as the rest of the world that needs what God has deposited in him.

## IRRATIONAL BEHAVIOR

I found myself counseling a beautiful young lady regarding her extreme defensiveness towards her husband in the midst of the smallest of issues. She was overly aggressive whenever there were occasions wherein they disagreed. She immediately concluded any disagreement to be authoritative opposition and an infringement of her human rights.

In prior relationships, she never allowed anyone to penetrate the protective wall she had built over the years. Now she was married to a wonderful husband who was becoming more and more concerned about her irrational behavior. They would get into heated arguments about things that really were not that serious.

It was in counseling I learned that she really loved her husband and knew he was a wonderful person, who looked out for her best interests. He was a marvelous father to her two children. One would never have known they were not his biological offspring. What was the problem?

The wife was desperate to save her marriage. She was willing to attend one of our Lifesavers Clinics, which focused on unlawful emotions. Almost immediately, she discovered that she was the problem. It was her mindset; her thought pattern regarding marital relationship.

She grew up in a household where her father was very controlling and abusive to her mother. She listened to his verbal abuse and even witnessed him physically abuse her mother. She saw her mother as helpless and stuck in a marriage simply for the sake of the children. She saw her mother struggle to get them out of the ghetto, while carrying the weight of a non-supportive husband.

As a child, just barely a teenager, she took a stance in her heart (soul) vowing never to allow a man to take advantage of her. Nor would she allow anyone to control her. Thus, at the first sign of disagreement in a relationship, her defenses would go up. At that point, every spoken word became the utterance of an enemy trying to break her will and bring her into captivity. She would explode and say things that were totally irrelevant to the situation. She was fighting for her mother. She was freeing her mother from fear and the possibility of any more abuse. It was not her husband she was battling with, it was her father.

As you can see, indirect experiences can have just as powerful an effect on us as direct experiences. I thank God for the knowledge of the truth. It saved their marriage and now she is able to counsel other young women suffering some of the same or similar dispositions.

## MINDSETS

A *mindset* is an established attitude regarding people, places, things, or issues. **Mindsets are formed by the method and elements we use to judge situations, circumstances and relationships, or simply, the way we process direct and indirect experiences.** A mindset then becomes the dictator of our actions or responses to the things we experience.

On a broad scale, we can look into the past experiences of some cultures and see how these experiences have formed mindsets that govern a whole nation. For instance, the Holocaust formed a "never again" mindset in the Jewish nation. Likewise, we can see how the mindsets of social groups changed history; for example, women's rights groups that fought for a woman's right to vote.

Each of us has mindsets formed out of direct or indirect experiences. In the darkest moments of my youth, a man walked up to me on the street, pulled me into his office, filled out some paperwork and in two days I was back in school on an OEO (Office of Economic Opportunity) scholarship grant. This changed my life forever. No, I didn't go on to get all the degrees that would have established me as an accomplished and distinguished citizen of this world, but it took me out of the environment and the dead-end street I was on. I was given an opportunity to see that I could do something important with my life.

But this direct experience also created a mindset in me that says, "Sometimes all the worst of us need is a little help, love or concern from our fellowman." Therefore, I have spent the last thirty-five years of my life reaching out to help those who seem beyond hope. The mindset I gained from this direct experience is to 'never give up on anyone.'

The question is, "Where do mindsets fit inside of our salvation?" A mindset is a manifestation of a spiritual disposition. It is a revelation of our true heart or desire. Whether good or bad, mindsets that were developed as a result of our exposure to direct or indirect experiences are not legal currency for getting into heaven. In truth, if a mindset was formed by a positive or negative human experience, then the same can surely change it.

Mindsets are a collection of human experiences that manifest identity and character. We are quick to conclude that only negatives mindsets are detrimental to our salvation. However, any mindset that was not formed as the result of a direct relationship with the Father, the Son and the Holy Ghost, is a manifestation of the influence of the flesh. Therefore, it is the mind of Christ we must submit to. His mind has no flaws in its thinking. This is not something that is so hard to accomplish.

We have been made one with God and Christ. We are in Him and He is in us. We have the mind of Christ and we can access it through simple obedience to the Word. To obey God's Word is to walk in the Spirit. Walking in the Spirit is a manifestation of our oneness with God and our Lord Jesus Christ.

I have often heard ministers say that God likes diversity; and that diversity was evident when He structured the Body. I totally disagree with this philosophy. Jesus prayed....

## John 17:11

*And now I am no more in the world, but these are in the world, and I come to thee. Holy Father, keep through thine own name those whom thou hast given me, that they may be one, as we are.*

## John 17:21-22

*²¹ That they all may be one; as thou, Father, art in me, and I in thee, that they also may be one in us: that the world may believe that thou hast sent me. ²² And the glory which thou gavest me I have given them; that they may be one, even as we are one:*

The answer to this prayer leaves no room for diverse mindsets in the Body of Christ. We all may have and exemplify many different natural preferences regarding personal likes and dislikes in responding to our physical environments, but our mind is one regarding spiritual things that influence the flesh.

We all have the mind of Christ. We all should have the same sentiments regarding one another and also the world. There is only one mindset capable of influencing the flesh that is lawful for the Sons of God

*"...Jesus saith unto them, My meat is to do the will of him that sent me, and to finish his work (John 4:34).*

# MEANNESS

We are the sons of God, created in righteousness and love. We have the express personage of Christ dwelling within. Yet many of us are mean and hateful in our dealings with others. We are offensive in character and indifferent in emotions. Are these the attributes of those who have inherited the divine nature of our God? I think not. But why are the saints of God mean? Beloved, hear me. For the saints of God, meanness is either learned or resurrected behavior. What do I mean by this? Simply that we who are born-again are new creatures; old things are passed away.

**I Corinthians 13:4-8**
>*⁴Charity suffereth long, and is kind; charity envieth not; charity vaunteth not itself, is not puffed up,*
>*⁵Doth not behave itself unseemly, seeketh not her own, is not easily provoked, thinketh no evil;*
>*⁶Rejoiceth not in iniquity, but rejoiceth in the truth;*
>*⁷Beareth all things, believeth all things, hopeth all things, endureth all things. ⁸Charity never faileth...*

One may ask the question, "Is it possible to be born mean?" The answer is yes. Those who are not of the righteous seed are born in sin and shaped in the iniquity of satan. This iniquity is manifested in many different ways and characteristics. Nevertheless, and most assuredly, meanness for the people of God is either learned or self-taught behavior.

According to the dictionary, ***heartless, callous, cruel, unkind, malicious and spiteful are all synonyms for meanness.*** Notice the first two, heartless and callous. Both of these suggest that meanness begins in the heart. I suggest to you that it is a disposition of the heart that is developed as a result of a decision to walk after the flesh in dealing with life's experiences.

In this chapter, I want to consider that many of the saints of God either know or are directly related to someone they would like to see delivered from meanness. Of course we know that the answer is salvation; which delivers and produces the character of Christ. However, many in our spheres of influence who are saved still come to us for counsel. Many live with spouses, parents or friends who are simply mean and hateful in their dealings with others. These saints do not know how to deal with such character, nor do they know how to counsel others who may be encountering the same.

It is important that you keep in the forefront of your mind the fact that saints of God, (the truly "born-again"), must train or rather retrain themselves to become mean and indifferent toward others. Since they are new creatures in Christ Jesus, this disposition is not inherent in them. It is a foreign mindset, an evil disposition of the heart and a cruel insult to the Father.

The simple resolution to such behavior, for the saints, is an obedient response to the chastisement of the Word, which demands they submit, repent and continue their walk in the Spirit. But for the benefit of learning how to minister to those who suffer as captives or victims of this mindset, we will discuss some root causes that will serve to identify the fetters that bind this spiritual disease to the saved and unsaved. The reason we are able to discuss meanness as captivity for the lost and a choice for the saint simultaneously, is because, once a son of God chooses to walk in the flesh, he or she will return to, or revisit, the character of the old man they once were. Therefore, for the sake of understanding, we will discuss this mindset from that perspective.

## LOVE AND AFFECTION

It is a natural instinct for all mankind to desire love and affection. Even God desires to be loved and affectionately entreated. When children grow up in an environment void of these elements, they are subject to respond with character traits void of love and affection. They invariably become mean and hateful.

There is an old saying which states, "You can't miss what you never had." This is not true. In many cases one can come to hate that which they never had. For instance, a child grows up in the environment mentioned above, void of love and affection. Yet, he or she is constantly surrounded by other families whose dispositions are just the opposite. The parents in these homes are kind

35

and thoughtful to their children. Even the people on the sitcoms are loving and caring. They are not indifferent or unconcerned. Although the child may love his or her parents, that love is stressed and strained as he or she tries to survive the parents negative mannerisms.

At some point in time, the child will reach a pivotal point wherein he could move in any spiritual direction capable of shaping his character for the rest of his life. He could become an introvert, not able or wanting to express the deep need or desire for love and affection. Oftentimes, these introverts are resourceful enough to turn rejection and indifference into hidden passages that allow them to travel deep into their soul, ending up in a place called 'the imagination.' Here they are safe from verbal abuse and rejection.

However, the imagination, as you will learn, is a place where another world void of God's influence can be created. It offers the introvert an opportunity to deal with those who rejected or were indifferent toward him, or to go even further in acting out bitter rage and violence. In some cases, such rage and violence is acted out in the imagination until it is presented with an opportunity to be lived out in the real world. This scenario is often manifested in the behavior of serial killers, rapists and murderers. We also see this in the psychotic behavior of schizophrenics.

**When meanness is a reaction to a lack of love and understanding, it is used to cover one's true feelings. It becomes the opposite of love. It is to be pettily bad-tempered, disagreeable and hard to cope with.** In other words, the lack of these human essentials gender meanness, which is really a façade and a mere hiding place to shield true feelings. One could become extremely hostile or violent, always looking for someone or something at which to strike. The lack of love leaves a void in us that cannot be filled by anything else. Nevertheless, we will try to find a substitute. For some, hostility, hatred, even violence is the answer. Could that possibly be the reason the love of God towards us is so effectual?

## WHEN MEANNESS IS LEARNED BEHAVIOR

The strangest fact about this mindset is that in many cases you may be more giving, kind and tolerant with those who are not intimately involved with you. But the one who shares your vows and your bed is the one you can't seem to give the benefit of the doubt. Why is this? It certainly seems the opposite would be true. Nevertheless, the sad fact is the spouse who offends in any matter is the one who receives the harshest punishment. But let's not stop there. It is also true that the spouse does not have to be offensive at all, to be victimized by this mindset.

The truth is, spouses, children, parents, or intimate friends are the ones who owe you love and loyalty, and they are also the ones who expect to receive the same from you. Here then is a ready-made stage for venting the mindset that was developed from the indifference or meanness you experienced as a child or from other relationships. You expected those in your past who owed you love and understanding to provide it. However, they failed to do so. Whatever the reasons were, they did not give you the love and consideration you craved. Therefore, you feel no one deserves to be given what they expect from you. You didn't get it, so why should they be so blessed by you. This is only one manifestation of this spiritual disposition. There are others.

## INDIFFERENCE

In some situations, children experienced parents who may not have been what we may define as mean, but who were extremely indifferent. The things that really mattered to the child were treated as unimportant and totally unnecessary. This indifference could have left the child in a **state of suppression**, causing him or her to become **introverted** and **repressed**. However, in some cases, the child began to strike back with rebellion in the form of meanness. You too, may have become indifferent to the situations and circumstances in the lives of others. You may not be sympathetic to their hurts or disappointments simply because no one regarded your pain or disappointments.

If you are not sensitive to the spiritual disposition of others *(Philippians 2:4)*, this insensitivity is a lack of love on your part. It will not allow you to empathize with the disposition of another, because to do so would be an act of mercy and grace. Since you believe no one provided you with mercy or grace (at the times when you felt you really needed it), you find it difficult to provide others with such affection.

## SELFISHNESS

On the other hand, the root of your meanness could be selfishness. In fact, you may be one who had very good, kind and loving parents. They could have been very conscientious of your every need. They may have been there when you needed them the most. They could have reached out to you in every way possible to make your life happy and full of joy. Nevertheless, you ended up meaner than a rattlesnake. Why? Maybe you are just plain selfish. Could it be you interpreted their love as entitlement? Perhaps you feel everyone should cater to your every desire. If so, you will most certainly attempt to take advantage of those who love you. You might even go so far as to verbally and/or physically abuse them.

**In addition, selfishness has no regard for the disposition of others. It is a watchful eye on the things that affect you and only you.** You do not care if someone else suffered or was displaced, as long as your desire was satisfied.

## SEXUAL FRUSTRATION

The root of your meanness could be sexual frustration. Many married men and women are experiencing the effects of the meanness of their companions due to a lack of sexual fulfillment. This is a real problem in the lives of the saints of God. The Church has refused to address this issue head-on, but it can no longer look the other way while marriages are falling apart and spouses hate the thought of each other.

If you are suffering from both a lack of affection and/or a lack of sexual fulfillment with your spouse, then you must learn to deal with this situation God's way. First, you must believe the Word of God has the answer that will deliver you from this anguish.

Secondly, you must realize it is the will of God for you to be satisfied sexually in your marriage. The Lord wants us to be happy. He knows that sexual frustration is the one thing that will make you most miserable in your attempt to serve and obey your husband, or to love and cherish your wife.

These frustrations can cause your heart to harden against your spouse and eventually destroy your marriage. You see, when the affections of the flesh are stimulated, they produce emotions in the heart. When the body is satisfied by the sexual act, it will cause the soul to be at ease and soothed. However, when the flesh is unfulfilled, it can cause the soul to be traumatized. This trauma causes the emotions to be disrupted. Therefore, the heart is not supplied with the necessary ingredients for producing a favorable emotion.

The love is there and the kindness is real, but the flesh is not brought to a point of fulfillment **or possibly** physical affection is nil. The husband may be totally selfish or unlearned as it relates to his wife's satisfaction. The wife on the other hand may be frigid and cold, without affection, and does nothing to stimulate her husband's desire for her. This can be frustrating.

But that's not the end of it. The added torment is that the saints know the laws of God forbid them to commit adultery and divorce is the controversy of the denominations. Therefore, they feel trapped in their marriages. They feel the matter is hopeless, and that the situation will never improve.

This seems such a damnable prospect. Therefore, the heart is hardened in order to protect itself from further disappointment. When this happens, you will turn to the only place you can find relief . . . the imagination. This is dangerous, however, because the imagination is capable of creating scenarios and sexual encounters that you will eventually seek fulfillment in the flesh through either masturbation or adultery.

In my upcoming book *"Saints and Sex"*, I will discuss thoroughly the captivity of sexual frustrations. Here it will suffice to say that you can be delivered from this hell. You can trust in the power of the Holy Spirit in your life. You do not understand all the ramifications of that statement yet, but I promise you the understanding will come as you continue to study the Thought War. For now, try to identify the root of your meanness. **Identification is ninety-nine percent of your deliverance**.

## UNFORGIVENESS

The root of your meanness could be unforgiveness. When you practice denying others affection or loyalty, unforgiveness becomes the ruler of the day. This is nothing more than wrong thinking that is allowed to destroy the love in your relationships. Frustration arises from the thought; *to forgive will not punish the offender enough and may gender an attitude of blatant disloyalty.* You feel you cannot allow that to happen.

To forgive might make you seem weak and frail in the relationship. Although you believe you will get some satisfaction from denying the offender a loving relationship, in the end you are the one who will suffer the withdrawal pains. This is masochistic and you will suffer the most. Why inflict this pain on yourself in the name of punishing others in your territorial sphere of influence?

Even in the case of marriage, though the Lord holds infidelity as a most legitimate ground for divorce, He did not wish to punish us by failing to apply grace in situations where we know that deep inside we still love and desire the offender. If he or she is willing to repent of the offense, why suffer the withdrawal pains? Why not forgive and come together again? Isn't that easier?

## THE PURPOSE AND EFFECT OF MEANNESS

When you are mean and hateful, you not only cause others to suppress their feelings for you, but you rob yourself of the supply of the very things you are craving: love, affection, kindness and consideration. You are starving for affection, yet you put up the facade of hard-heartedness to cover up your real disposition.

This mindset could cause others to feel unimportant and unworthy of consideration by you. They will begin to feel inferior to you, and will submit to your control in order to be considered by you. They too desire and need your affections. This can even lead them into a state of lowliness and depression. They will feel as if there is nothing they can do to please you. Therefore, they could label themselves as useless to the relationship and even to society itself.

Even if your meanness is just a cover-up for a feeling of rejection and past offenses that have never been dealt with, it can have a tremendous effect on the ones who love you. It could even lead a weak mind into committing suicide.

## RETRIBUTION

You may seek satisfaction through retribution for the indifference you experienced from others in your past or present life. This retribution may be derived by simply enjoying the power you have over the emotions of another. They desire your love and understanding, but there was a time when you desired the same from them or someone else. Now it is your turn. You are now in control of the emotional desires of another. Now you can cause someone else to feel what you felt. You could not do it to the ones who disappointed you in the past, but now you are in control. You have decided to be mean and hateful, disagreeable and indifferent.

**Meanness is not captivity for the sons of God; it is a choice.** However, it can be selective, purposeful and calculated. (Selective means it chooses the ones on which to perpetrate evil). Remember, meanness is learned behavior; you can select the people you will be mean to. Many children observe their parents being kind and loving at church among the saints, but mean and hateful at home. A husband may be patient and tolerant of others, but totally impatient and unyielding with his wife and children.

A wife can be loving and kind to her children, but mean, hateful and forever unforgiving of her husband. The objective might be to hurt or punish the husband for offenses or his failure to cater to her needs. However, when he does cater to her, it is never enough.

Remember, you have denied someone of love and kindness. You have refused to be sensitive and considerate. You are disagreeable and hard to get along with. Consider that when you deny another of your love, understanding, consideration and sensitivity, you also stop them from expressing their love for you. You cause them to suppress their love, while they search for a way to deal with your disposition. Therefore, you can no longer feel their love. So what do you get for being mean; only the satisfaction of knowing you have hurt others.

**Meanness is a blatant display of your pride, self-righteousness and idolatry.** Once I knew a minister who was also a businessman. But his character was one of meanness and hatefulness toward his children, his daughter-in-laws and even his grandchildren. After attending one of my conferences, he became convicted and after much counsel, he finally apologized to them for his unrighteous attitude. However, it became apparent the apology came about as a result of momentary fear, because soon afterwards, he was back in full ungodly character. It was so easy for him to berate those who really loved him. The fact some of them worked for him in the family business did not make things any better.

One day, one of our senior bishops confronted the elderly minister again about his meanness. He replied, ***"You have to be mean in business."*** Consider the content of this remark because it expresses the mindset of many Christians. It says we can treat others like garbage simply because they work for us, and this of course is all right with God. When you are out of character, walking outside the boundaries of the faith, you will convince yourself of the most ludicrous things.

One day one of his sons said to me, "He makes my wife and his granddaughter cry all the time. I think he really enjoys doing that." The moment he spoke, ***the Lord said, "That is the truth, meanness does enjoy hurting others."*** I cringed when I heard that. These individuals worked for him. Therefore, he thought nothing of talking down to them and saying malicious things he knew would hurt their feelings. After all, he is the boss, the supreme one. He pays them and they need him. Therefore, they must bow down and accept the humiliation or be gone.

This is pure meanness and hatefulness. However, it is also selective. I noticed that one daughter, who is very vocal and does not work for him is not treated in such a manner. This daughter speaks her own mind and does not acquiesce to anything she does not agree with coming from the father.

By her own testimony, the house she grew up in was void of love, compassion and consideration. Instead, it was filled with judgment and cold discipline. She was always belittled and criticized. However, she met the Lord and is born-again. The power of her salvation and the truth she has learned helped her to overcome the offenses of her past by forgiving her abuser.

This is a classic example that confirms meanness as learned behavior. The daughter who we will call Wanda, and the father whom we will refer to as George, had been in the household of faith for more than twenty years when I met them. After sitting under the truth a few weeks, Wanda began to see that her character had traits of meanness and self-righteousness. She realized that she had installed in her own character some of the attributes of her Father. This convicted her and she hastily sought to purge herself of this unrighteousness.

The first step to her deliverance was to admit her true disposition and accept the fact that it was not pleasing to God. Out of concern for her soul and not wanting to hurt others the way she had been hurt, she changed. She is more loving and considerate of others now. She and her husband are closer and he is enjoying her new, more loving disposition.

Though Wanda learned meanness during the years she lived with her father, she was able to destroy that influence simply by agreeing with God. You can do the same.

George, on the other hand, remained stubborn and unyielding. He worships his power and authority over people and continues to demand they submit to his control. The Lord sent me and at least six other ministers to plead with him to submit to the truth. Nevertheless, he is convinced his charitable deeds will cancel out his lack of godly character.

This case was amazing to me because George knows all the facts. He knows none of his family members want to deal with him. He knows he is unable to get any of them to follow him to church. He knows that after more than thirty-five years of salvation, he has absolutely no spiritual influence in their lives. What is more mind boggling is that he knows he has not walked in the character of Christ. He knows he is mean. These things he has confessed openly. But pride and self-righteousness are strongholds in his life.

While writing this book, the Lord impressed upon me that George's time is running out. Soon his heart will cease to beat and his eyes will cease to open. Unless there is strong intercession going up for him, these spiritual fetters will never be broken and he will surely end up in hell where his soul will be eternally damned. Stop and say a prayer for George. The Lord knows him. He is your brother in the Lord. Ask the Father to be merciful enough to bring him to true repentance and humility.

# REBELLION

Sometimes meanness is nothing more than your rebellion against the wrongs or denials in your life. You can break free of this mindset. Consider how you felt when you were disappointed by people you loved. Let that be the measuring stick for the way you deal with others. Remember the love they have for you, and don't allow your meanness to destroy that love. Don't pretend you don't care. You do care. Everyone wants to be loved.

**The key to your deliverance is vulnerability.** You must be willing to become vulnerable again to the people in your life. You must learn to trust the hand of God. He demands you love openly, but He also knows you may get hurt in the process. Therefore, He installed in the act of love, the ability to heal itself. Don't be afraid to love freely again. The power of your own love will heal you, even if you do get hurt. Don't keep pushing your loved ones away with your temperament. Don't send them away with your hurt and unforgiveness. You need their love. You crave it. Don't forfeit it. Whatever the problems, they can be solved. Don't let it be too late in your life. Do not live in a world of hate and despair. Break out of it and begin to love and consider the ones who love you. Remember, love suffers long and is kind. It is your only hope.

*Father,*

> *I thank you for revealing to me the inner workings of meanness and how it affects those, I love. Teach me, Father, how to forgive and to pray for those who have hurt and despitefully used me. Perfect*

*love in me, God, so I will not be selfish in my dealings with my fellowman. I will learn to love them the way you have loved me. You have loved me unconditionally in spite of my deficiencies. Cause me, Father, not to look at others after the flesh, but to discern the disposition of their hearts, which will reveal their love and concern for me. Help me to allow this lesson to become a part of my life. Thank you for your loving kindness and your patience towards me. I will forever give you the praise.*

*In Jesus' name,*
*Amen.*

# JEALOUSY

Jealousy is the one mindset that has done the most to hinder the peaceful progression of the human race, as well as the spiritual movement of the Body of Christ. It is being skillfully used to stop the flow of love and to destroy the unity of the Faith.

The Bible declares there is no power that is not of God. He ordains all power, good or evil. This includes thrones, kingdoms, principalities, dominions, governments and civil authorities, as well as socio-economic position.

**Romans 13:1-2 (AMP)**
*1 Let every person be loyally subject to the governing (civil) authorities. For there is no authority except from God [by His permission, His sanction], and those that exist do so by God's appointment.*
*2 Therefore he who resists and sets himself up against the authorities resists what God has appointed and arranged [in divine order]. And those who resist will bring down judgment upon themselves [receiving the penalty due them].*

Since it is God who gives authority, power and position it is profitable for us to submit to those instituted authorities. This would be not only for fear of the wrath of God, but also for conscience sake.

What does this have to do with jealousy? Everything! *Jealousy* is **resentment or suspicion of anyone who is believed to have an advantage you do not have**.

I have encountered those who were jealous, resentful and extremely bitter against those who have or appeared to have advantages they did not possess. This does not even have to be real; you might just think they enjoy an advantage that you do not have. **A universal operation in every case of jealousy is that it seizes any opportunity to blatantly or subtly discredit or destroy the reputation of another.** Any opportunity you have to make the one you are jealous of look bad, you will take it. The purpose is to draw attention to you. We can see this operation in families, corporations, organizations and yes, even the church.

The motivation for jealousy could be fear of rejection or most of all, the fear of losing your uniqueness inside of your territorial sphere of influence. This disposition can be caused by ignorance or spiritual immaturity. You may suffer feelings of rejection from those you love or admire, or feel you have to perform perfectly in order to be accepted by people. On the other hand, you may also feel you are only accepted because of your ability or the things you can accomplish. Whether true or false, in your mind people never really love you for who you are. You see their relationship with you as fake, while there are others in your environment that the same people tend to love and respect, even though they may not be of good character or have the abilities you do.

## JEALOUSY IS ALSO HATRED OF GOD

If someone is enjoying an advantage you do not have, God gave it to that individual. You must see that God allows them to have that position in your life. If you are jealous, it is because you hate what God is doing in someone else's life. Someone on your job may receive a promotion you feel you deserve. You become jealous and frustrated because you have not discerned or accepted that God is exalting that individual. Once again, you have not agreed with God. He allowed this situation to reveal the true disposition of your heart. Consider the following scripture:

**James 1:17**
*Every good gift and every perfect gift is from above, and cometh down from the Father of lights, with whom is no variableness, neither shadow of turning.*

If you are jealous of someone's abilities, then remember every good gift comes from God. If you are jealous of someone else's accomplishments, remember it is the Lord who exalts. If you are jealous of the good that is accomplished in someone's life, then you are resentful of God the Father, for it is He who causes the just and unjust to prosper.

Earlier, I stated that the motivation for jealousy is the fear of rejection and of losing one's uniqueness inside of a territorial sphere of influence. I want to explain this further by using the conflict between Saul and David. In the Old

Testament, the Lord rejected Saul as king over Israel because of his disobedience. As part of his chastening, the Lord informed Saul that He would raise up a man who would be better than he. Since David was the one God chose, Saul began to hate David.

In looking closer at the spirit of jealousy in this scenario, we see that Saul was brought face to face with his sin against God long before David's anointing for kingship became an issue. Saul knew he had dishonored God and that the Lord's rejection of him as king served as punishment. Since those were the facts, it is obvious Saul knew that David had nothing to do with the Lord's decision (1 Samuel 15:24-26). Why then did Saul develop such venomous hatred for David? To the naked eye, it would appear that Saul hated David because of the favor David had with God.

If we look a bit closer, we will discover that Saul did not simply hate the person David, as much as he hated the Lord's presence in David's life. This can be seen in the overall relationship Saul developed with David over the years. He made him head of the Israeli armies, gave him his daughter to marry and treated him as a son. Yet, in one moment when the people sang, "Saul slew his thousands and David his ten thousands," Saul's whole countenance changed against David. Iniquity entered his heart and jealousy dominated him resulting in hatred and violence. How could one feel such adverse emotions toward another person or how could one's feelings about a person change so quickly? Jealousy is as cruel as the grave (Solomon 8:6).

David never did anything to hurt Saul. He always reverenced him as God's anointed. Even when given the chance to kill Saul, he did not. All that Saul experienced in his relationship with David was good. He knew also that David's heart toward him was pure because it had been demonstrated time and time again.

How can you hate someone who is good to you?

**Proverbs 6:34-35**
> *34 For jealousy is the rage of a man: therefore he will not spare in the day of vengeance.*
> *35 He will not regard any ransom; neither will he rest content, though thou givest many gifts.*

Again, the answer to this question may shock you. The truth is Saul hated the Lord's presence in David's life. He knew the Lord was working with David in all that he did. The same security he once enjoyed was now gone having been given to another. Saul was losing his uniqueness among the people. He knew the works David did were the works of the Lord being accomplished through him. Saul's anger and displeasure was really towards God for having chastised him for his disobedience. Saul hated the fact that the Lord rejected him. In essence, he hated God.

When you hate another without a cause, it is usually due to (a) some natural or spiritual failure on your part, or (b) a fear of losing your uniqueness. This is how Saul felt when the women sang the song comparing his accomplishments to those of David. David was now in the picture and was capable of doing things just as well and even better than

Saul. Saul had lost what he felt made him acceptable or unique among the people. On top of that, he had to carry the burden of knowing that he had been rejected due to his own failure to obey God.

## JEALOUSY HAS TO HAVE AN EARTHLY TARGET

David was a visible representation of what Saul hated. It was impossible for Saul to take vengeance on the Father; therefore, his anger and hatred fell upon the one whom God had favored. Saul hated David without a cause and consequently moved into open rebellion against the Lord. The Lord was the target of Saul's resentment, but this resentment was ventilated through jealousy of His visible representative. Saul wasted so much time and energy fighting a battle he could not win. The earth and the people on it belong to God and He can give whatever He wants to whomever He wants (Romans 9:17-33). Who is able to stop Him? What Saul should have done was humble himself by accepting the judgment of God and be thankful that God did not kill him on the spot. Saul should have agreed with God.

Jealousy must have an earthly target to war against. Though the motive for the war is hatred of God, the battleground is the relationship and the prize is the discrediting or slandering of the one being used by God. It may not always be a saint whom God chooses to exalt within your territorial sphere of influence. Nevertheless, their exaltation will reveal your true spiritual disposition.

## JEALOUSY IS CRUEL AS THE GRAVE. IT PERVERTS EVERY EMOTION, DESIRE AND REASONING

If you are jealous, you will not refuse an opportunity to avenge self. You will always look for a way to get even, discredit, dishonor and hurt those of whom you are jealous. Jealousy will cause you to devise (to form, plan or arrange in the mind) evil imaginations (Proverbs 6:18). The attributes of jealousy are hatred, hostility, legalism, pride, unforgiveness and judgmentalism. To walk in jealousy puts you on the enemy's turf and makes you vulnerable to these attributes. You must see the evil of jealousy and just how devastating its effects can be. You must not forget it was jealousy that caused Lucifer's heart to be filled with iniquity and hatred toward God.

Many people have physically harmed and even killed others because of jealousy. I have counseled husbands who were so jealous of their wives; they made their lives a living nightmare. Many had no reason to be jealous, as their wives were faithful and doing all they knew to be godly women. Their husbands, however, were filled with suspicion and evil imaginations that were not real.

I am reminded of a young man who would watch movies in which women were unfaithful to their husbands, and then get so angry with his own wife because he thought she too, was possibly being unfaithful to him. He would become enraged to the point of physically harming her. However, her unfaithfulness was only in his mind. His wife constantly tried to reassure him of her faithfulness and love for him, but that did not help. His thinking was irrational, unreasonable and outright evil. No matter how caring and loving she was, he was still suspicious, jealous and hard to live with.

I have also known women who have made those around them miserable because of their jealousy. There was a young lady who would sit in the service and watch her fiancé the entire time to see if he was looking at any of the other young ladies. She could not focus on the Word or any part of the service because of her possessive nature towards her fiancé. She also cheated herself out of possible friendships with other women in the congregation because she was constantly wondering which one of them wanted her fiancé.

The situations stated above were very tormenting to those involved. These people were in a no-win situation. Imagine every day of your life being filled with suspicion, resentment, pride, unforgiveness and hatred. These mindsets caused both the perpetrator of such evil and the victim to suffer. They were kept bound to an endless cycle of despair and hopelessness. But praise God they were able to be set free through Jesus Christ!

## JEALOUSY CAN PRODUCE SPIRITUAL HYSTERIA

The marriage of a Christian couple in corporate America ended in divorce; but how did they get there? The wife's commitment to God and hard work enabled her to build quite a large business before she married. The people who worked for her knew she was honest and fair in her dealings with them and they loved her for that reason. After she married, she brought her husband into the business and pretty much allowed him to run it. Unfortunately, he was not as committed to working the business as his wife, but wanted to reap all the benefits it afforded him. Furthermore, the employees respected him as their boss, but knew he was just an opportunist who only wanted what he could get out of the business.

There were times when the business would endue pitfalls and profit losses. Then the wife would consult the Lord and gather wisdom as to how to pull out and turn things around. The employees and all who knew her considered her to be a smart businesswoman.

Soon the couple began to experience turbulence in their marriage. The husband became grossly unfaithful and the wife was very aware of his infidelity. It was obvious he had no respect for the sanctity of the marriage, his wife's pain, or the stumbling blocks he placed in the way of those he chose to become his victims. (Remember they were both born-again believers in Christ). In spite of the truth he knew, he had a mindset that said, "I'm just being a man." The wife, on the other hand, was very spiritual and would never think of cheating on her husband. Nevertheless, over a period of years, the husband became even bolder and the women he dealt with became more and more disrespectful to his wife. This he allowed and even sanctioned.

At some point in the chaos, they found their way into my conference room for counseling. In the session, the husband did not deny any of the accusations the wife leveled against him. She continued to pour out her heart, citing how she had done all she knew to do. She had given him everything: the highest position in the company, authority and money. Even though he conceded all this to be true, it was clear that he had deep resentment for her in his heart.

I had several other sessions with them both after that and faithfully the roots of bitterness were exposed. The bottom line: the husband was raised in a family where he literally adored his father, who was the pastor of a church, while the mother was given charge over the children. She was also the one who executed most of the discipline in the house. He had several sisters and brothers of which he was the eldest. He described his mother as mean and hateful in her dispensing of discipline and her authority to forbid them to do things or go places.

The father was a very dominant figure and did not believe women were to do anything beyond serving the husband and raising the children. He was from the school of thought that barred women from any decision-making processes in the home and certainly, she was to keep silent in the church.

The young man quickly adopted this belief system and admired his father for suppressing his mother and sisters. He was most happy when his father denied his mother of something she wanted to do. But his joy was often short-lived, because she would take her frustrations out at the whipping post whenever he broke the rules. This made him more and more resentful of her. However, the resentment ran deeper than that of a child's anger about a whipping.

He hated her. She was a woman, a lesser vessel, but she had authority over him. He was the eldest of all the siblings and they all watched as she humbled and humiliated him. He was seventeen years old, nearly a grown man; yet, she still had authority to veto anything she did not think he should do or be a part of.

He told me of a time when he wanted to play in the high school marching band. He came home with his uniform all excited, really believing his parents would be proud of him. When his mother saw the uniform, however, she was livid. She informed him in no uncertain terms he was not going to be in any band. Surely his father would stand up for him and override her, he thought, but that did not happen. She made him take the uniform back to the school and turn it in.

Some of his siblings made fun of him and laughed about it. He was devastated. Ashamed and heart-broken, he obeyed, but never forgave her for that day. Fifteen years later, it was just as painful when he spoke of it, as if it had just happened.

The tone in his voice and the spirit in which he spoke of her, both suggested a deep resentment. The truth was he hated his father as well. Why didn't his father recognize that he was old enough to be taken out from under that woman's authority? Why did he force him to submit to her?  Even though he wanted to be like his father, he hated him for not exalting him above the authority of his mother.

This is a classic example of jealousy.  The young man resented his mom, true enough, but he also resented the one who gave his mom power over him.  He was jealous of his mother.  She enjoyed an advantage he did not have; she had his father's ear.  Her word carried more weight with his dad than his and there was nothing he could do about it.

The same is true in your spiritual walk among your brothers, sisters, friends and foes.  If you are carnally minded and perceive any of them to have an advantage or privilege you do not share, jealousy is imminent.  But it doesn't stop there; you will also resent the God who gave them that advantage.

What does all this have to do with the young man's infidelity?  Well beloved, just connect the dots.  When the young man came of age, left home and went out into the world on his own, the roots of bitterness went with him.  Any woman having authority over a man became as his mom.  His wife was smart and powerful.  Besides that, she had accomplished some things he had never accomplished.  People loved her and looked up to her in a way they did not regard him.  In spite of the fact his lack of integrity was the reason people didn't hold him in as high esteem as they did his wife, she was the target of his resentment and the image that had to be destroyed.  In business, she was smart and powerful and there was no way he could compete with her in that arena.

But he had an ace in the hole. She loved him and he could use that love to break her. She was too high and mighty. He wanted to bring her low. All the love he felt for her was buried now beneath the iniquity in his heart. She enjoyed respect from the people in the company and all their friends. But he was going to show her what it felt like not to be loved and respected; and he would use other women to do it.

As a result, he involved himself in one affair after another, not really caring whether she knew or not. This was more than simple lust; it was also retaliation. He was getting back at his mom and every other woman who dared to go beyond serving her husband and taking care of the house. He wanted to break his wife. He wanted her to feel low and unimportant. He wanted her to feel what he felt; so his affairs progressed to encounters with riotous women who had no qualms about disrespecting his wife. He enjoyed their intrusion into her world. He liked the fact that she was saddened by his indiscretions. He hated her. He needed to bring her low so that he could feel taller.

In all his endeavors, however, he forgot one thing. His wife knew God in a real way. God was her Comforter, and so she was able to overcome every offense. She survived the ordeal without becoming bitter and vindictive. She understood his need to control her; he had nothing that was truly his. It all belonged to her. Once again, here was another woman with more power than he had. Though she loved and pitied him, he could never overcome his lack of self-worth. Eventually they divorced and went their separate ways.

God never intended for our relationships with each other to be grievous or tormenting. Love is liberating. It does not seek to place one in bondage. We must also bear in mind that although the people around a jealous person suffer, the one who is jealous suffers as well. They are in bondage and are unable to love as God designed us to.

Our heart toward them must be tender, understanding and patient. We must see them as souls whom the Father loves, even when their negative deeds are directed at us. When a jealous person is at their worst, we must show them the love of God and trust that love to do an effectual work in their life.

## YOU CAN OVERCOME JEALOUSY

You must first admit that you are simply jealous. Ninety-nine percent of deliverance is identification. As long as the enemy can keep you in a state of denial, deliverance will not take place.

*Confess your faults one to another, and pray one for another, that ye may be healed. The effectual fervent prayer of a righteous man availeth much (James 5:16).* Despise the shame, and humble your heart before God and man.

Submit yourself to the cleansing power of the Word. Speak the truth in love, so you can grow up in all things, even into Christ. The Body of Christ is fitly joined together and each joint is compacted with that gift, knowledge or talent it is to supply. If each member is able to supply the thing

God gave them, the body would be able to edify itself and increase in love (Ephesians 4:15-16). Rejoice at the well-being and doings of others. It is the Father who promotes or abases.

Communicate with God. He will lead you into your place and work with you there. You are important to God and that is all that matters. The Father is a Comforter, but we must make ourselves vulnerable to the Holy Spirit and confess our jealousies to God.

Stop trying so hard to maintain the image of yourself that you have established or want to establish in the minds of others. This will not work in the Kingdom of God. You cannot serve God while trying to make a reputation for yourself.

## BECOME A DOER OF THE WORD

Identification and confession are great; however, they will profit you nothing if you do not put the Word of God in action. It does no good to know what to do, but never do it. The knowledge of God must be applied in your every day walk. For example, scripture instructs us to think on those things that are lovely, pure, just, true, honest and of good report (Philippians 4:8). These must not be mere words, but you must do it. Your thoughts must remain inside these boundaries. To think otherwise opposes God and will always lead you into sin. The Father placed boundaries on your thinking for your own protection. He knew just how far into sin an evil imagination would carry you.

In order to change negative feelings about a person, your thoughts about that person must first change. When your thoughts change, your feelings and actions will change as well. It is impossible to love someone you think evil of. I have counseled saints who struggled with loving people and found that, in most cases, they were trying to love people with their actions, but something different was in their heart. Their imagination was filled with evil thoughts concerning those they were trying to love. The heart was not in agreement with what the flesh was outwardly doing. This kept them frustrated and defeated in their Christian walk.

## BRING EVERY THOUGHT INTO THE OBEDIENCE OF CHRIST

Wrong thinking is the root of all sin. So a man thinketh, so is he. You are what you think. Begin to monitor your thoughts and cast down every one that exalts itself above the knowledge of God. Consider 2 Corinthians 10:

> *4 (For the weapons of our warfare are not carnal, but mighty through God to the pulling down of strong holds;)*
> *5 Casting down imaginations, and every high thing that exalteth itself against the knowledge of God, and bringing into captivity every thought to the obedience of Christ*

This is powerful! The indwelling Holy Spirit gives us the ability to bring every thought into the obedience of Christ. We are in control of what we think. When an evil suggestion is presented, it is within our power to refuse to entertain it. Just as we choose to think evil, we can also choose to think righteously. We must resist the temptation to think evil thoughts. Remember, happy is the man who is able to resist temptation.

Staying before the Lord in prayer and reading the Word daily will help you to retrieve your mind. It must be constantly exposed to the truth. This is so important. You will never bring God glory with an evil imagination. Obedience to the Word of God is your way out of agitating passions and the miseries of sin. It is also your way into fellowship with God and benefiting fully from your salvation.

Put your confidence in God, knowing that He loves you and is able to change you. Determine in your heart to renounce (give up) all feelings of jealousy and resentment. Learn to be content with the gifts, talents and abilities that the Father has given you. Accept who you are in God and trust His will for your life. God wants us to love one another, but this will never happen if we do not deal with the sin and iniquities that keep us separated. Agree with God.

# OBSESSION

In the secular world, there is a very popular fragrance called *Obsession* that has a sweet, distinct aroma. However, spiritual *obsession* is **a poison that leads you into an emotionally persistent pursuit of an idea or feeling**. This idea or feeling is <u>birthed in the imagination</u>; thus defining the Biblical terminology for this mindset: to imagine. An obsession is the mental force by which a created image in the mind drives the flesh to limits, striving to fulfill the requirements of the image. This poison causes blindness to reasoning, and **will deny any communication that seeks to change the mindset.**

Those who are obsessed are willing captives of an idol, which may be a person, persistent idea, desire or an emotion that cannot be removed by reasoning or logic. **Obsession is a mindset that results in compulsive preoccupation, total delusion and lying emotions**. The reasoning faculty shuts down and one will not entertain anything that does not enhance the obsession. <u>One may hear the truth but will not allow it to have an effect in their life because of the blindness of the heart and dullness of hearing</u>.

**An obsession is also a delusion in which the created image (idea, personal disposition, desire, emotion, etc.) is accepted as fact**. Though the imagery is a lie, it is accepted in the mind as real. The fact that the image created may or may not be obtainable by the flesh is of no consequence to an obsession. In the imagination, that which is not yet accomplished in the flesh is virtually forced by the soul (heart) to be accepted in the mind as reality. This is because the heart or soul never allows the mind to see any obstacles able to hinder the vision. To the mind, they simply do not exist.

**Ephesians 4:17-18**
> *17 This I say therefore, and testify in the Lord, that ye henceforth walk not as other Gentiles walk, in the vanity of their mind,*
> *18 Having the understanding darkened, being alienated from the life of God through the ignorance that is in them, because of the blindness of their heart:*

**Blindness of the heart is also evidence of an obsession.** The driving force of the obsession overtakes all the emotions, desires, appetites, imaginations, and will. The emotions are given over to feeling only those things that enhance the vision. Oftentimes, this is where the truth is denied. Truth or reality has challenged the validity of the image, which the mind has already accepted as truth regardless of what the facts are. Therefore, any attempt to discredit the vision must be met with strong opposition. It then becomes easy to hate anything or anyone who interferes with the furtherance of the illusion. The fruit of this operation is hardening of the heart against obvious truth. You become as a mule, stubborn and obstinate. You become determined to have your own way. In other words, you begin to kick against the prick thus causing self-inflicted pain.

# OBSESSION WILL BLIND YOU TO THE TRUTH

Many have built worlds around their illusions. If you are not honest in your assessment of your own spiritual location, you too, could create an imaginary world in which a desired feeling or belief is "Lord and Master." There are many who are perfectly happy living in their world of falsehoods. If you consistently tell yourself a lie, you will begin to believe it. The obsession that the Church has today with the acquisition of things must be constantly fueled by the old Faith and Prosperity Message. This *"name it and claim it"* jargon has developed a mindset that is not the mind of Christ. Any other mind that is in us, however, other than the mind of Christ, shall be revealed according to *Philippians 3:15*. This is evidenced by the most recent challenges to the validity of the Faith and Prosperity Message. The believers of such a doctrine are sometimes vicious in their defense of it. They don't want to hear the truth, even though that message has never delivered all that it promises.

Do you remember the life of Saul, who was later known as the Apostle Paul? He was obsessed with binding the saints. The letters of permission to persecute the saints, which he received from the high priest, fueled the mindset that he had received from his traditional teachings. Saul was on his way to Damascus when a light shone from heaven and caused him to fall to the ground. Jesus then introduced Himself to Saul who submitted to the Lord and asked, "What would you have me to do?" (Acts 9:1-5).

If you notice, the Lord did not send Saul back from whence he came. He knew that Saul's traditional mindset could not serve Him. However, if we really look into the mind of Saul, we will see that he really believed in what he was doing. He trusted that his actions were pleasing to God. This brings us to the realization that the motivation for an obsession is not always one of evil intent. But what was the danger of this obsession, especially when the intent was not evil? The danger was the fact that Saul would not hear the truth. He was present at the sermon in which Stephen superbly put the Old Testament into proper perspective. This really should have gotten his attention, considering he was an expert on the Old Covenant. However, the truth did not move him. Saul had a one-track mind that insisted on believing that anything contrary to, or outside of, what he had learned had no merit. That is the problem with an obsession; it shuts down the ability to reason, even while hearing the truth. It will deny any communication that defies its own conclusions.

## THE DRIVING FORCES IN SOME OBSESSIONS ARE POWER AND/OR CONTROL

What was the real obsession in the case of Saul and his persecution of the church? Was it the fact that Saul simply believed in the traditions of Judaism, or was he obsessed with destroying anything that opposed his belief system? I venture to say that he was obsessed with destroying the opposition to what he believed.

I know that Saul or rather Paul considered himself a contender for the faith of Judaism. As noble as that may seem though, we must stay true to the principles of discernment. I suggest Paul was obsessed with the Christians and he wanted to destroy them and their faith. He saw them as traitors to all that he held dear to his heart. The thought of their betrayal of his God and his beloved Judaism (to which he had devoted his entire life), was unconscionable, and morally unacceptable.

Now we begin to see the power of an obsession. It will blind you to the truth. If Paul only regarded the will of the Father, and had his heart been open to receive from God, then he would surely have responded differently to the message Stephen preached. But he was obsessed with having his way with the Christians. This obsession blinded his heart and closed his ears to anything that opposed his desire. We can see then, that the destructive nature of an obsession is the desire to control another's actions, beliefs, or convictions. Could that be the reason Jesus had to knock Saul off his mule and bring him down to the ground before he could speak to him?

The letter Paul obtained and carried with him to Damascus was the symbol of the power that fueled his violent and destructive nature. But it was the obsession itself that revealed his violent nature. Thus, we have another reality to examine...

## OBSESSIONS REVEAL TRUE CHARACTER

Saul took pride in the fact that he reverenced the Law of God and was extremely devout in his commitment to those laws. However, he still possessed and maintained a violent, unforgiving, hateful and destructive nature. How could this be? The truth is, oftentimes, <u>one's true character is suppressed until the soul discovers a desire that will satisfy a perverted will</u>. Where there is opposition to acting out the mind's conclusions those violent and destructive emotions are triggered.

This also proves that the Law of Moses had no power to deliver a man's conscience unto righteousness. Neither could the law reveal Saul's violent nature. In fact, the legalism in the law served to enhance it. This is quite contrary to the operation of the Holy Ghost in the dispensation of Grace, wherein any mind other than the mind of Christ will be revealed (Phil.3:15).

## HATRED IS BRED IN AN OBSESSION

We have seen Saul's denial of the truth as preached by Stephen. Even though Stephen was preaching under a heavy anointing, it did not move Saul or the men of the city to belief. Instead, it made them angry enough to kill the man of God. This is another devastating attribute of an obsession. <u>It will breed hatred in the heart against those who would try to bring the Word or any truth into the midst of the obsession</u>. Over the years, I have been the victim of much hatred as I have tried to counsel saints out of their obsessions. If one is not really seeking to please the Father, then he will fight to hold on to the obsessions of his mind. Because some deny the power of God and reject the counsel of the Holy Spirit, they have no godly purpose to drive them. They promote the illusions of their imagination to the forefront of their existence and spend a great percentage of their time considering how to implement their will.

## OBSESSION ACCEPTS NO DEFEAT

An obsession is an illusion. It is only real in the individual's imagination. However, those who are obsessed, see the illusion as something they can accomplish. There is never a moment when an obsession allows you to concede to defeat.

If the obsession is an idea, then the idea must live; if it is a feeling, then the feeling must be maintained. You must win the cause, you must accomplish the goal. Every detriment is considered an act of war. Anyone who tries to destroy the vision becomes the enemy, whether it is the Word of God or God Himself. This is the destruction in an obsession.

As truth becomes the enemy and the object of resentment, so are the truth-bearers and he who is the source of truth. The Lord being the author of all truth becomes the unfair intruder in the mindset. Truth brings unwanted light to the inward parts and challenges lying emotions. Since denial of the truth cannot entirely extinguish the light of truth, confusion becomes the disposition of the soul. Confusion is also an invader in the private emotions of the obsession. The truth, which caused the confusion in the first place, must now be dealt with severely. It receives the harshest of punishments. It is more than rejected; it is converted by the mind into a lie. The truth that opposes the obsession must be sacrificed in order for the obsession to live.

# OBSESSIONS DO NOT ALLOW REPENTANCE

Reasoning must also be denied in order for an obsession to live. Those who are obsessed will listen to the truth but will never hear it with their heart. An obsession can hold you captive in such a way that you will not be able to see past your desire, idea or the person with whom you are obsessed. Many are not able to do the work of the Lord because of their obsession with someone or something. Many Christians are in this state.

**Hebrews 12:16-17**

> *16 Lest there be any fornicator, or profane person, as Esau, who for one morsel of meat sold his birthright.*
> *17 For ye know how that afterward, when he would have inherited the blessing, he was rejected: for he found no place of repentance, though he sought it carefully with tears.*

One must be careful not to come before the Lord with an Esau spirit. Note that Esau's tears were due to his loss of the blessing. However, in his heart, he never repented for having offended God. This is the detriment of an obsession. Its blindness to the truth will not allow you to take full responsibility for the consequences of your actions. You may be sorry for the consequences but may not admit to your own mind that you are the cause of such results. Instead, you will blame whatever or whoever becomes the agent of reality. **Hatred then builds for those who oppose your will, even the Father Himself.** Yes, many hate the

Lord today because He has not allowed their obsessions to be fruitful. To the obsessed mind He becomes the enemy. You may never verbalize this; nevertheless, the mindset is true.

I have conducted many counseling sessions over the years involving men and women who were extremely obsessed with their own ideas, people, desires and even a gift in ministry. One such case comes to mind...

## DEBORA

I think one of the most interesting and bizarre obsessions is when one is obsessed with his or her self. Debora was obsessed with her perception of herself. Her image was her number one idol and her desire to be rich and famous followed closely behind her obsession with authority and control. Those whom she worked with, her children and even her spouse characterized her adult life as mean and hateful. Looking into that life, it was obvious that she was very unhappy in her marriage and the dead end street she thought to have found herself on. But lo and behold, ministry was supposed to change all that. But when she found herself faced with the same martial issues she had endured for so many years before, she became bitter and even more self-serving. All she wanted was to make her own mark. She became obsessed with making a name for herself. She resented the fact that her position or station in life was tied to her husband. Her face became set like a flint to become the woman of her imagination, successful, famous and wealthy. The wealth would guarantee her power, control and independence.

No matter how much truth she learned, Debora was determined it would not deter her from reaching her goals. Nothing and no one would get in her way. People in her life became a means to an end. The ministry God gave her became leverage to use in manipulating the saints into giving into her bosom. But obsessions often, as in this case, lead to other unspeakable sins. She became an expert at using feigned words that bewitched the people of God. They fell under the spell she cast with pretense, lies and perverted truths. She could manipulate the saints into believing anything she said. Even when they didn't believe her, she could get them to do whatever she wanted. That is the amazing power of ministerial witchcraft.

But not only were her words feigned (pretense), but her deeds as well. They were calculated and designed to make the saints believe she had certain sentiments she really did not possess. I thank God for the power of the Word, because many have been delivered from this spell and are able to identify its tentacles in their lives and the lives of others. Some had to be counseled against harboring bitterness and resentment, but the power of the Word in their lives has made them free from the devices of satan.

Nevertheless, Debora's obsession survived despite the fact she understood the consequences of doing despite to the Holy Ghost. When the grace of God exposed the tactics used against the saints, she refused to submit to the chastening of God and simply left the ministry she was in and went to start another. In doing so, she freed herself from the righteousness of God she had preached to others. This is sad because the wrath of God will be revealed against all ungodly men and women who hold the truth in unrighteousness. Those who do such things will suffer severe chastening or worse will find themselves given over to their own mind. Debora's obsession has hardened her heart against the ways of God. She is no longer sensitive to the truth. She is altogether free from righteousness. This simply means the truth regarding her negative behavior is without conscience.

Repentance is more than words; it is the act of returning to the will of God. It is submission to the way of God. It is relinquishing our way and accepting His way. Debora's lack of remorse for the deception and abuse she inflicted on the people of God has fortified her pride and caused her to become spiritually blind to the truth. She does not believe that hell is her destiny, if she does not embrace the truth God has exposed.

The obsession will not allow Debora to see that she is not really competing with men or women, but with the design the Holy Ghost has set for her life. I pray God will not turn her over to her obsession, because the end of it is eternal damnation.

## OBSESSIVE AND COMPULSIVE LYING

There is a reason Paul wrote, *Lie not to one another, seeing that ye have put off the old man with his deeds (Col 3:9).* Our former master, satan, is the author of the lie. Those who lie are advocates of his objectives. The purpose of a lie is to deceive, to paint a false picture of something or someone. It is designed to mislead and misdirect.

## Proverbs 6:12-19

*12 A naughty person, a wicked man, walketh with a froward* (perverse, deceitful, lying), *mouth.*

*13 He winketh with his eyes, he speaketh with his feet, he teacheth with his fingers;*

*14 Frowardness is in his heart, he deviseth mischief* (evil) *continually; he soweth discord.* (strife, calamity, trouble, chaos)

*15 Therefore shall his calamity come suddenly; suddenly shall he be broken without remedy.*

*16 These six things doth the Lord hate: yea, seven are an abomination unto him:*

*17 A proud look, a lying tongue, and hands that shed innocent blood,*

*18 An heart that deviseth wicked imaginations, feet that be swift in running to mischief,*

*19 A false witness that speaketh lies, and he that soweth discord among brethren.*

It does not matter what you confess to be if your actions place you in the middle of the scriptures above. As far as the Lord is concerned, you are evil and perverse in your ways. To make matters worse God classifies you as a lover of chaos. That means you enjoy causing strife in relationships, stealing the joy of believers, killing the spirit of the innocent and destroying the peace among the saints.

Let us stay with the facts here. Jesus said, *"The thief cometh not, but for to steal, and to kill, and to destroy: I am come that they might have life, and that they might have it more abundantly* (St. John 10:10). We cannot escape the fact that such character is that of satan. Many saints are used by him to be spiritual thieves in the congregation of the people of God. Could this be their purpose for being in the church? Again, let us keep the facts straight.

From the leadership's perspective, it would be the desire of the pastorate to bring such souls into spiritual perfection; for this is the will of the Father for our life. From their own perspective, however, pride and hard-heartedness has opened the door for them to be consumed by their obsessions and the need to sow discord among the saints.

One might wonder, "Why do they continue to come to church?" Especially when it is obvious, that it is their obsession with chaos that leads and guides them. They have created a vision in their imagination regarding the destruction of others; including those leaders who have continuously counseled them. They want to see them fallen and humiliated. Like satan, they want to gloat at their demise. They are obsessed with seeing the people of God placed in predicaments that belittle them before all who holds them in high esteem. They work to see them discredited and brought to an open shame. This is what they live for. They fantasize about it daily; and their daydreams are consumed with it. They are lost and completely given over to satan. As long as these obsessions live in them, they will always be an adversary of the gospel of Jesus Christ.

Consider those who reside in your sphere of influence. Can you identify those who may have made themselves willing captives of their obsession with causing chaos in and among their family, friends and even the church?

In order for them to break free, they must first admit that the obsessions are real. Then, they must renounce all the hidden things of dishonesty lurking in the heart. They must repent of the evil they have wrought in the lives of the people of God and seek forgiveness. Perhaps the Lord will pity them and extend His mercy.

We must continue to pray for them as many have great spiritual potential. If they would hear truth and obey counsel, they would have a chance to live a productive life in God. But if they continue to nurse their obsession, the ditch they dig for others will surely become their own grave.

## EXCHANGE OF INFLUENCE

It is necessary for us to discover how to get saints delivered from their obsessions. The truth is deliverance from all sin is accomplished in the same manner. One must simply, repent (renounce and turn away from the sin), submit to God (the heart must change and it will, if you simply agree with God), and walk in the Spirit (if you walk in the Spirit, you will have the emotions of the Spirit).

An impression must be made in the heart and on the fleshy mind that is more powerful than the obsession itself. In the case of Saul, it was the supernatural visitation of Jesus. This made an impression that was more powerful than his desire to destroy the Christians. The heart and mind must be introduced to something more impressive than its present desire. It must be provided with something else to love, consider, and entertain. When this happens, the obsession is purged.

There must be an exchange of influence. In the exchange, one must be willing to embrace that new idea, feeling or truth. Saul demonstrated this when he humbled himself and asked of the Lord, "What would you have me to do?" Since he obeyed the vision and proceeded to walk in the way of instruction, he was able to experience the love, mercy, and overwhelming grace of God. These were things he had never experienced under the law.

But note, Paul was only afforded this opportunity after he obeyed. Many are never delivered from an obsession or any other negative mindset, because they never allow themselves to experience the attributes of God. If there is never an understanding of that which is holy, which is the Spirit of Knowledge, there is nothing else powerful enough to adequately impress the soul or the fleshy mind.

David said, *"Oh taste and see that the Lord, He is good!"* Until one embraces the Word, which is God, there will never be deliverance from any obsession or any other negative mindsets. Our obedience to the Word of God causes the Father to reveal Himself to us. Only then will one experience His love that surpasses all understanding, His faithfulness, security, and comfort, knowing that the Master is always present and that He will never leave nor forsake us.

As powerful and captivating as an obsession may be, the way out is always the same. Submit to the Word and agree with God. When He forbids you to have something, agree. When He instructs, obey. When He directs, follow. Hear the Lord and agree with His will for your life. **The power of obedience is far more powerful than any obsession.** It allows you to truly experience the love of the Father. It is when we obey the Word and agree with the will of God, that our paths are made straight and our way is filled with eternal peace.

1. Beloved there is no magic formula; nor is it hard to achieve total freedom from the bondage of sin of any kind.
2. You must face the destructive nature of the obsession.
3. You must also agree that the fanaticism of your actions is fueled by a desire to obtain or maintain power or uniqueness in a situation, circumstance or relationship.
4. You must admit that this driving obsession has made you void of all reasoning or submission to obvious truths.
5. I encourage you to try the one thing you have never experienced: obedience. **Obey the Word of God.**
6. I guarantee the Lord will meet you in the midst of your mindset and help you destroy the power of obsession.

We are the sons of God. Our deliverance is within us. For the Word is nigh unto us, even in our mouth and in our heart. Obey that Word and hear the counsel of the Lord. The joy you will experience in doing so will be your strength to walk in the Spirit.

# OVERCOMING FRUSTRATION

<u>Frustration</u> is a mindset birthed out of spiritual lack and **erroneous interpretations of life's experiences**. The word itself has the following meaning:

(1) To bring to nothing, to stop short, refusing to go on and to be filled with dissatisfaction due to unresolved problems or unfulfilled needs;
(2) It is blighted hope or failure of expectation;
(3) Frustration is a mindset that says "forget it" and
(4) It is also a mindset that keeps an individual from ever coming into the fullness of his or her ministry or learning contentment in all things.
(*Dr. Banks' Expository Dictionary*)

Many saints become very frustrated with themselves when they cannot seem to move ahead. Untiringly, they spend hours trying to do the things they believe will motivate God to move on their behalf. Frustration and discouragement then begin to evolve when God does not move and all their efforts seem to be futile.

You may be serving very faithfully in your local assembly. You may even be involved in the administrative duties of the church, give to charities, say all the right things, pray and even fast. However, you must realize these things alone will not motivate God to move in your life. It is a righteous purpose and a pure heart that gets God to move for His people.

Frustration will keep you from ever understanding your experiences. But without *experiential knowledge*, there can be very little, if any, spiritual growth. The following is a list of some of the situations or circumstances that may cause frustration in your life.

## TRIALS AND OFFENSES

Often, painful, fleshy and emotional afflictions are not attributed to the work of the Holy Ghost in building character. Instead, it has been conveniently laid to the charge of the devil. It is religiously acceptable to believe that the enemy is working against us and interfering with our acquisition of natural things.

Apostle Paul told us in Philippians that he learned how to be abased and how to abound. His circumstances never changed his love for the Father. He had <u>peace</u> and <u>contentment</u> in whatever state he found himself.

Can you truly say you are not resentful of hard trials and tribulation? You see, you have plans and strategies that do not include some far-out trial that serves to disrupt the flow of things. It simply has to be the devil working against you.

**Here is the truth: Tribulation works patience and the trying of our faith is more precious than gold.** <u>These are the principles we cannot afford to forget when trials</u>

come our way. Jesus said that trials or offenses will come and all who name the name of Christ would experience them. I remember Jesus saying things to the disciples and then explaining why He told them the things He did. *And now I have told you before it come to pass, that, when it is come to pass, ye might believe (John 14:29).* This is the principle you should keep before you.

**The Word of God reveals the truth regarding things you will experience in your walk of faith**. These things are revealed as principles that must be fulfilled in every believer. The Word speaks to you of the trying of your faith; and then the trial comes. This forecasting was done so that you might believe and know that the Father is mindful of every experience you encounter.

Why are you so frustrated with trials and offenses? Do you not read the scriptures? Are you not attending a church that teaches the principles of our faith? Or perhaps you are simply ignoring the truths you have learned. In any case, *Beloved, think it not strange concerning the fiery trial which is to try you, as though some strange thing happened unto you: But rejoice, inasmuch as ye are partakers of Christ's sufferings; that, when his glory shall be revealed, ye may be glad also with exceeding joy. If ye be reproached for the name of Christ, happy are ye; for the spirit of glory and of God resteth upon you: on their part he is evil spoken of, but on your part he is glorified (1 Peter 4:12-14).*

The conclusion of the matter is this. Either you will embrace the truth in the passage above, or you will continue to walk in frustration, feeling sorry for yourself and blinded by trials that are meant to confirm the effectual work of grace in your life. Agree with God and you will begin to experience the peace of God in the midst of each trial or offense.

## HOPE DEFERRED

I have seen so many people become frustrated from having embraced promises made by men in the name of the Lord that were never fulfilled. Many have stood on a word spoken to them, confessed it and believed in their hearts that God was going to perform some materialistic miracle. But, because it was not in His purpose for their lives, it never happened. *Hope deferred maketh the heart sick (Proverbs 13:12).* **When something you expected to happen does not happen, the soul becomes sick with disappointment and frustration.**

Many have prayed for the sick and afflicted, believing in the healing power of God, but do not realize that He often heals according to His purpose and sovereignty. Therefore, when the sickness progresses or the sick person dies in the midst of all the praying, trusting and believing, the believer is left with no recourse but to try to justify why this happened. However, without a revelation of the truth, their explanation adds confusion to the situation. Consequently, they become frustrated and oftentimes offended with God.

## THE PURSUIT OF PROSPERITY

Millions of saints have given substantial offerings expecting God to reward them with tremendous financial returns that just never seem to materialize. They ignorantly continue to believe this to be the method God wants to use to give them the wealth of this world. <u>The truth is you have no right to believe God for something He never promised you</u>.

Some of the wealthiest businesses in the world are religious organizations. However, the Holy Ghost will not use false doctrines and erroneous mindsets to bring universal prosperity to the household of faith. Instead, the Church is charged with setting things in their proper perspective.

The saints of God are to give generously and freely to the gospel of the Kingdom. If there were a formula for acquiring the wealth of this world, saints would be the richest people in the world today. This is not the case. As a result, many saints have become frustrated with formulated religious rituals given to us in the old *Faith and Prosperity* message that do not work or bring relief to their situations. Many are left with unresolved issues that traditional church sermons are unable to deal with effectively. The end result . . . frustration in the Church!

The Body of Christ has finally begun to re-examine the **Prosperity message** that has led it into wantonness and false hope for the acquisition of things. The Church has grown sick of the promise of a blissful, wealthy existence on planet Earth during this dispensation. The sad reality is that the Church really wants to believe in this false

91

doctrine, although down in its inward parts it senses that such doctrines might not be true. This is evidenced by the work of faith in the life of the believer. It guarantees that any mindset other than the mind of Christ will be revealed *(Philippians 3:15).*

## PROCRASTINATION

Procrastination makes you non-productive both naturally and spiritually. It brings progress to a halt; which can and will have a domino effect on so many things you need to accomplish.

Procrastination is not always a result of laziness, although very often it is. Procrastination can also be the offspring of fear. Some fear facing the situations they have no control over, while others fear tackling tasks that could result in failure of some kind. The problem is they are pessimistic. This is so sad because these individuals will never know what the outcome could have been had they completed the tasks required. In many cases, the frustrations they suffer could have been avoided had they trusted God beyond their ability to assess the situation or work out the thing they desired to accomplish.

Procrastination in cleansing yourself from sin can also bring frustration. Many try to clean themselves up in the prayer closet. Yes, prayer is necessary. One must seek out the forgiveness of the Lord in order to walk out of any sin. However, the manifestation of purging can only be seen in the midst of trials. A clean heart is seen in the midst of situations, circumstances or relationships, not inside the prayer closet alone.

## ERRONEOUS BELIEFS

Some of the things you strongly believe may not be the mind of God. If this is the case, cause your heart to hunger and thirst after righteousness. God promised to fill you. When the truth comes, receive it with gladness. Jesus said we must believe as the scripture has said. The error in your belief system is not going to change God or the truth. But if you choose to hold on to your traditions, you will live a life of frustration and torment, never able to please the Father.

## STRIVING

Your frustration with job, family, friends, finances or ministry may be caused by your **lack of knowledge or submission** to what your role in each of these situations is supposed to be.

You should be a *peacemaker* in every situation or relationship. This means you will **in no way interfere with what the Holy Ghost wants to accomplish in any area of your life or in the lives of others**.

**If there is frustration in any area, it is because you are striving to make your will survive.** Think about this carefully. You may be doing all that you can in a situation and, still, it does not seem to change or may even get worse. You may seem handicapped in other areas and cannot even do those things you know you are capable of doing. It might be true that if you are not able to do what needs to be done, there will be great loss, hurt, disappointment or some other negative occurrence. In either case, it is time to stop and come to reality: **you belong to the Father and He is in control of every area of your territorial sphere of influence.** He knows the mental and spiritual disposition of all those you must deal with. He also knows the needs in your life.

## CONTENTMENT IS THE ANSWER TO FRUSTRATION.

Why has God prolonged the circumstance that have kept you aggravated, unsure and upset? Listen to the testimony of the apostle Paul in Phillipians 4:

> *11 Not that I speak in respect of want: for I have learned, in whatsoever state I am, therewith to be content.*
> *12 <u>I know both how to be abased</u>, and I know how to abound: every where and in all things I am instructed both to be full and to be hungry, both to abound and to suffer need.*

How contrary this is to what is being taught in the Body of Christ. Paul is saying that it does not trouble the Father for His children to be <u>abased</u>. The Greek word used here is *tapeinoo:* **to make low, bringing to the ground or a humble condition.**

Paul goes on to say he is **instructed to be full and to be hungry.** What does he mean when he says, "to be hungry?" Will God allow His people to live such a life? Yes, He will! He will take you through periods of materialistic and physical need. Why? So that you might know Him as a provider of all those things necessary to accomplish His will for your life and to maintain a holy walk in this perverse world. More importantly, you will experience the greatest attribute of all: GOD'S FAITHFULNESS. For it is at those times that patience can have its perfect work, as you receive strength to go on in the power of His Might.

**James 1:4**
> *But <u>let patience have her perfect work</u>, that ye may be perfect and entire, wanting nothing.*

You are not responsible for making any matter a success. This is the responsibility of the Holy Ghost. Yes, you may see that someone or something is going to be lacking if you or someone else does not succeed. This can cause you to become really frustrated with God's people. However, your charge in the situation is to give it all that you can physically and spiritually. **Make sure you maintain a righteous motive and a spiritual disposition that remains within the boundaries of the faith.** Once you have done this, it is the responsibility of the Holy Ghost to take the situation to the end. If things seem to be lingering in disarray, look inside of each situation to see what the Lord is trying to teach you about Him or yourself. **It is most likely that He is using the circumstance to develop patience, love or sensitivity in you.**

## Matthew 6:33

*But seek ye first the kingdom of God, and His righteousness; and all these things shall be added unto you.*

**The Kingdom of God is righteousness, joy and peace in the Holy Ghost** (Romans 14:7). If these things which pertain to our spiritual or natural livelihood are intended for us, then why don't we have them? Why is the Church so frustrated when God has promised these things? Did God lie? Would He have us frustrated and not able to <u>trust</u> His Word?

The Word of God declares that we must first seek His kingdom and His righteousness, and then <u>all</u> ***these things*** shall be added unto us. This is where the problem lies . . . relative to the things promised to us by the Father. If we keep this passage in the context in which it is written, we would discover that the <u>things</u> referred to here are listed in the 31<sup>st</sup> verse:

## Matthew 6:31-33

*31 Therefore take no thought, saying, **<u>What shall we eat?</u>** or, **<u>What shall we drink?</u>** or, **Wherewithal <u>shall we be clothed?</u>***
*32 (For after all these things do the Gentiles seek:) for your heavenly Father knoweth that ye have need of all these things.*
*33 But seek ye first the kingdom of God, and his righteousness; and all these things shall be added unto you.*

The Father promised to give us **food, drink** and **raiment. This is all that is necessary for the preservation of the flesh to do His will.** However, this passage has been presented to the Church as a supernatural gathering of the wealth of this world to be given to the saints of God. **But what happened to godliness with contentment is great gain**? (I Timothy 6:6)

Because this is not the dispensation for the wealth of the world to be given into the hands of the saints, many have become <u>frustrated</u> waiting on such blessings to come. They do not realize that will never be the case, until the dawn of the new millennium in which the Master will return and set up His Kingdom on the earth. <u>It is then, that we will rule and reign as the head and not the tail in this great plan of God</u>.

**For now, the Kingdom is the domain in which God resides with His righteousness within our hearts.** When our hearts are moved toward God in holiness and righteousness, He is then motivated to move for us by providing those things needed to preserve the flesh for service. Don't allow erroneous interpretations of your experiences to produce **frustration**, rather than **contentment**, in the midst of situations or trials.

There are many ministers who are not willing to withdraw from doctrines that are not scriptural, go back to their congregations and confess their errors (even after being instructed by the Holy Ghost to do so). If they would submit and confess their error, the Holy Ghost would smile on them and prepare them all over again to be used in His eternal purpose. Because this is the case for so many, they will have to miss this move of the Holy Spirit and watch the new generation that is fearlessly submitting to the revelation of the Kingdom message.

Beloved, don't let this be your end. Submit to God. Shake off the world and worldliness. Be content with righteousness and the things the Father blesses you with. Fill your inward parts with truth, and I promise you will be able to face whatever is ahead in the days to come.

# FRUSTRATION AND SELF-RIGHTEOUSNESS

Frustration can be the result of self-righteousness and unresolved sin. You may desire to get back on course with God, but are hindered because your heart is not in the right place with His people; or you may find in the midst of sin, that you are able to see the negative effects it has on the people around you. Yet, pride will keep you from doing what is righteous in resolving the problem. Therefore, God will not afford you forgiveness nor bring deliverance in light of your pride.

If you continue to walk among the people you have offended without acknowledging your wrong, you are training yourself to be arrogant. God will not bring you out of that sinful situation until you have fulfilled the righteousness of true repentance. In the meanwhile, you may become extremely frustrated with the manifested consequences of the sin itself.

Let me make this very clear. Many times individuals are sorry for the consequences of the sins they commit. However, they are not sorry for committing the sin itself. You see, the consequences may cause you to be denied some things you really want. **When sorrow is due to personal or materialistic loss, it is not repentance.** True repentance is gendered when one considers his relationship with God at risk.

If God removes you or others from a situation, for the sake of those affected, that does not mean you are delivered from the sin. In such a case, the move of God is for His people in spite of your selfishness. If you continue in your sin and do not heed that small voice within, deliverance will not come and your frustration will continue to build. ***Forgiveness will only come when the love of God fills your heart for the victims of your offense.*** It is very frustrating to seek forgiveness for sin and find all your efforts are fruitless. Your heart must be in the right place with people in order for forgiveness to come from the Father.

**Frustration causes you to do nothing.** You can frustrate the grace of God when you become complacent, selfish and arrogant. <u>In the midst of circumstances, situations and relationships, faith needs to operate</u>. However, if you do not examine your heart for motive and true disposition, repentance for sin will not be found. For example, if you really want deliverance, you must despise the shame involved in humbling yourself and asking God and man for forgiveness. Faith without works is dead.

The best way to handle frustration when you are burdened with unforgiveness and guilt is to deal with the situation head on. Do what the Word says. When you obey the Word, you change. When you change, the situation has changed.

**Confrontation is the catalyst for change**. Once you confront the situation and acknowledge the wrong, you will feel a release of the burden. Open confession is not always confessing to an entire congregation. Open confession is to go back to the situation or relationship and confess your wrong to those involved. If you continue to disobey that still, small voice, you will be inhibited in moving ahead in God. You will not move spiritually until that voice is answered.

## Romans 10:3

*For they being ignorant of God's righteousness, and going about to establish their own righteousness, have not submitted themselves unto the righteousness of God.*

Another cause of frustration is the desire to establish your own righteousness inside a situation, circumstance or relationship. This is called self-righteousness. When you fail to submit to God's way, you will always experience frustration. <u>Remember, the Lord will allow you to encounter negative circumstances, situations and relationships to reveal your mindsets.</u>

You must always judge what you feel in everything that is set before you. Judge righteously, checking to see if you have dishonored anyone in a situation. You must never be *presumptuous*, thinking that because your heart is pure and no malice was intended, that the other person was not offended. Always consider the spiritual disposition of another.

**Self-righteousness is also a result of judging others by your own standards**. Tell the truth and tell it to the ones who can benefit by it.

A few days before the release of this book, I noticed I had a missed call on my cell phone. I recognized the name on the caller ID and immediately checked the voicemail to see if the caller had left a message. Well, there was a message, but I am sure the caller didn't intend to leave it.

Apparently she had dialed my number by mistake and when I didn't answer my voicemail picked up. She and another veteran leader were in a car looking for an address in the town where they lived. While doing so, they began to talk about the disposition of people in their local assembly, including the leaders.

The recording was several minutes long, but the gist of one's concern was *'members of the congregation forming opinions of you based upon what they have heard, without knowing the whole story.'* She rehearsed how leaders *need to have wisdom too*; implying that the one they were referring to just didn't have any. The other minister in the car with her was obviously in agreement and offended by those who stand on platforms that do not reach out with love. She went on to say *that stuff doesn't just blow over etc, etc, etc.* But interestingly enough, she also stated how in such cases *you are expected to be all loving, and self-righteous when you come around that individual.* In other words, you've got to fake it.

As I listened to the recording, I could hear the bitterness and resentment in their spirit. Even if all they said were true, the bitterness in their souls negated any righteousness on their part. The tone they spoke in was that of malice, resentment and jealousy. I wanted to cry. I said, "Lord, these are veterans of the faith. But they are so carnally minded and malicious. They are in no way able to help the situation." They themselves are standing on platforms that do not attempt to reach out with love, mercy, grace or truth to those they deem as off course. Instead, they buried that opportunity in the bond of iniquity, false loyalties and self-righteousness. They are not worthy to judge others regarding the lack of love, because their own hearts are full of darkness.

These are people in the Body of Christ, in whom sin is lurking at the door of their mind, waiting for an opportunity to manifest itself in the flesh. The Holy Ghost is a <u>discerning</u> Spirit and will always reveal your true mindset. **Self-righteousness is an attempt to cover your wantonness and ways of the world**. It is a powerful resistance to the Word. **It is strengthened by religious jargon and uses the Word for its covering.**

## SELF-RIGHTEOUSNESS IS BLINDING

**The amazing thing about self-righteousness is its ability to blind its victims to the truth.** After more than four decades of ministering, I have found it to be easier to deliver fornicators, adulterers and witches, than those saints who suffer from self-righteousness. Even though they are the most frustrated people in the church, being hard workers, striving to reach goals that always end in failures and disappointment; they just never seem to get it. They never connect the dots. God never allows their agenda to prosper, even if it is a righteous agenda. They never accomplish it because their work is done in iniquity.

Even though they have witnessed it repeatedly, they just don't get it.

A man or woman could fall into sin causing pain and disappointment in the lives of others. But if that individual truly repents, God will continue to use him or her in His reformation. Some judge this falsely because they might have seen the individual fall more than once. But what they refuse to judge is that when the individual gets back up, he or she is able to do well in ministry. The people who witnessed the fall continue to love them, and the Lord continues to use the individual in a way that all must testify it is the Lord. The self-righteous never accept the fact that God judges the **content** of an individual's heart at the moment of repentance. Even if in the future, the individual falls again, at that interval their heart was pure toward God and man.

## SELF-RIGHTEOUSNESS PUTS YOU ON YOUR OWN

Self-righteous saints do not understand that when they fall they struggle to get up because they never go to God with a clean spirit and a pure heart toward His people. There are always elements of resentment and iniquity in their soul. And because they don't enjoy the quick restoration that another may receive, they become frustrated, angry and malicious in their thoughts regarding those who find favor with God.

# SELF-RIGHTEOUSNESS IS FORTIFIED BY PRIDE

Self-righteous individuals never judge themselves justly. They always make allowances for a little leaven. Their spiritual dispositions are fortified by their pride. This keeps them from ever meeting the requirements of humility. They walk on in the pride, struggling with life and pushing away the helping hand of God.

I counseled a minister once who had resentment and iniquity in her heart against two other ministers. In the scenario, they were all guilty of something. So I told each of them individually what they needed to do to satisfy God's requirements. Well, the two immediately humbled themselves to the one and apologized for the breach in their relationship. They begged to move on in righteousness. But the one was hard-hearted and merely said all the right things. It was obvious her spirit was not in agreement with God.

The Lord sent me to her again and I called her in for more counseling. I told her the Lord's mind and she agreed with me. She promised me that she would go to the other, humble herself and make real peace among them. But, of course, the image of herself which she worshipped religiously, would not allow it. Things in her life began to deteriorate more and ministry became an afterthought. Months later she called one of the other women saying that she had been in prayer the night before and God said she needed to call her and apologize. Wow, what a revelation! He only said it over and over again several months prior.

Nevertheless, this was an attempt to appease the conscience who knows that righteousness had not been achieved in the situation. How long will it take for the young minister to contact the other woman and humble herself? But more than that, who knows whether God will even tarry with her any longer. Her pride is an affront to the Lord. It has devastated her ministry, buried roots of bitterness and infringed upon her anointing. I wanted to go to her and plead on God's behalf again as I had done several times before. But God said, "No. She has to receive or reject me now." I was so afraid when I heard this. A year has passed and she still refuses to humble herself to that particular person (whom, by the way, God is using mightily in ministry).

Self-righteous people do not see God through the impurities of their heart; so the best they can do is sit back, judge, criticize and look for fault in those whom God is using. They are quickly becoming spectators, who had their spot, blew it, but would never truly repent. They are as Esau in the wilderness peeping at the Jacobs who inherited their blessings; the same Jacobs who caused them much pain and heartache but wrestled with God until they changed.

If you are one who walks in self-righteousness, learn from this chapter. You may not be a minister but these principles are the same in any situation.

# OVERCOMING DEPRESSION

Whether saint or sinner, when natural emotions for the unsaved or spiritual emotions for the saved; are not expressed, opinions or true beliefs are not voiced and desires are not lived out in the body, they remain in the soul to be lived out in the imagination. The imagination then produces an even stronger desire for the emotions to be expressed by or through the flesh. The continuous denial of these God-given expressions can lead to severe depression. This suppressed state can be caused by many different situations, circumstances or relationships. However, regardless of the root, suppression will lead to severe depression.

Depression is a state of despondency or dejection (sadness), which arises from feelings of severe hopelessness, inadequacy and despair. It is to accept a lying reality of having been forsaken. These feelings are extremely excessive when compared to the situations or circumstances from which they were birthed. Depression is an abandonment of God and His promises. It places you in a world void of God's power or presence. It is not a condition to be pitied or nurtured. But must be dealt with for what it is; a cruel and unfair behavior that puts our God to an open shame.

But how do the sons of God fall into this abyss called depression? As in all captivities of the soul and body, the child of God must first deny the Word of God and walk outside the boundaries of the faith. I cannot express enough the fact that it is impossible to walk in the Spirit of God and be depressed. This is a fact that cannot be ignored. If there is to be any deliverance for the people of God or the world for that matter, we must examine thoroughly the route a soul travels from being the light of the world to living in the deep darkness of depression. As always, the scriptures are faithful.

### Luke 11:33-36

*33 No man, when he hath lighted a candle, putteth it in a secret place, neither under a bushel, but on a candlestick, that they which come in may see the light.*

*34 The light of the body is the eye: therefore when thine eye is single, thy whole body also is full of light; but when thine eye is evil, thy body also is full of darkness.*

*35 Take heed therefore that the light which is in thee be not darkness.*

*36 If thy whole body therefore be full of light, having no part dark, the whole shall be full of light, as when the bright shining of a candle doth give thee light.*

First, depression is a spiritual condition. It is not of the faith, nor the Kingdom of Light; therefore it is devilish and of the darkness. It is due to failure to keep one's eye (spiritual sight or vision) on things pertaining to godliness. It is a forsaking of the influence of grace and the purpose of life in Christ.

When the eye is single we are able to walk in the benefits of the gospel of Christ. One such benefit is the knowledge that we are able to do all things through Christ who strengthens us. **There IS nothing in the will of God we are unable to perform**. Therefore, we can only be rendered helpless when we attempt to do those things that are not His will. Here is where we lose confidence in Him; knowing we are not in agreement with His purpose or design for our life.

You may think you are not able to identify with these truths because you are often depressed, but are not committing sins of the flesh. But I caution you on this wise, unbelief is sin. There are those who are depressed in ministry, wanting to accomplish ministerial goals that always seem to be out of reach. We may think such a one is to somehow be commended for their desire to do good. However, your desire cannot supersede God's purpose, method or timing. He is the guide. We are the followers of His wisdom.

**Depression is the result of a lack of faith.** When the realities of life's situations are too intimidating to face, these situations or circumstances must somehow be removed from the thoughts. This might be difficult though, if our daily activities are such that these intimidating situations are ever present. Therefore, an eventual physical shutdown is on the way. Suddenly you are too tired to get up or go out. It becomes almost impossible to properly function in your environment because much of your mental faculties are held captive by fear. It is the fear of thinking on those things that were taken from reality and hidden in the depths of the imagination. Therefore, there is only a small percentage of the mind left to process what is going on around you.

**Lust for things of the world can cause depression.** When the eye is evil, or rather when we forsake Christ and turn in pursuit of the things of this world, then surely darkness will consume our whole being. Oftentimes, the pursuit of our dreams and aspirations are met with fierce opposition causing delay and even impossibility. Thus, hope deferred makes the heart sick.

When the eye is not single, the whole body is full of darkness. Those who depart from the path God placed them on are blind and cannot see where they go. In some cases, one might wake up to this reality, knowing that he has lost direction and the ability to accomplish his or her dream. At that point, the right and righteous thing to do would be to return to the Father in repentance. But either stubbornness, pride or both mandate further vain efforts to accomplish the desire of the heart. These vain efforts could lead to depression; a world of darkness perpetuated by the fact that he or she is aware of the abandonment of God's purpose for their life. The acquisition of all the riches in the world will not remove that truth. They will simply be wealthy and depressed knowing God is not pleased with them. If such a one does not quickly repent, they will remain in this state of despair with nothing to look forward to except the indignation of our God.

## SUPPRESSION CAN CAUSE DEPRESSION

The human vessel has a built-in desire to give and receive

love, affection, consideration and kindness. When involvement in circumstances, situations or relationships form a mindset that denies expression; or the receiving of love, kindness and affectionate touch; suppression rules the relationship.

The word *suppression* means **to hold back or deny expression and thoughts.** There are many reasons that may cause suppression of your innermost feelings or thoughts. Regardless of the reasons, suppression is one of the most common causes of depression. However, I need you to remember, these are all conditions and operations of the flesh. They do not exist in the one who walks in the Spirit of the Holy Ghost.

In severe cases of suppression, the mind seeks to defend itself by turning against the flesh. Because the flesh is unable to provide an outlet for the emotions, it becomes the enemy in the *thought war*. The mind or soul seeks to maintain its supremacy by labeling the flesh as guilty, useless, lonely and not worthy of affection. This is true depression.

DEALING WITH AUTHORITATIVE FIGURES IN YOUR LIFE CAN CAUSE SUPPRESSION. For instance, many children live a life of suppression because their parents do not allow them freedom to express themselves. The child is therefore trained to simply respond to parental authority, without ever being given a platform to voice his opinions, feelings, or emotions concerning things that affect his life. In some cases, the child's suppressed emotions or thoughts are pushed so deep inside, they seemingly cease to exist.

The child can grow up in a situation like this and become so programmed that he will not voice his true feelings, for fear of punishment or rejection of some kind. This programming leads the fleshy mind to conclude and accept the situation as *"just the way things are."*

The fleshy mind may then accept what used to be "just the way things are" as "the way things ought to be." If this is the case, the mind has to bury the emotional pain that goes with suppression, as well as bury the suppressed thoughts themselves. This burial becomes so deep that these thoughts cease to exist as reality to the individual. In other words, these feelings are buried so deep, that you will feel as if the mindset that has developed from suppression is really your true character. This is a lie. **Your true character is hidden beneath the suppression**. You really want to express your emotions, voice your opinions and display your desires, but the authorities or situations in your life simply will not allow this. Therefore, you have submitted to suppression.

What you have now is simply learned behavior. Therefore, you may in turn raise your children the same way. You may be authoritative without listening to the mental disposition of your children. This is why many teenagers are committing suicide. They feel they have no one to talk to, when it is really their parents with whom they cannot communicate. This suppressed state is what makes them vulnerable to any lie the enemy will perpetrate.

Suddenly, there is no one in the world for them. No one understands and therefore, no one cares. Life seems useless and meaningless. <u>The suppression has now progressed into depression</u>. The heart has fainted. The emotions are exhausted. The will to live is broken. The imagination is filled with the image of a worthless, no good person who is undeserving of love and may no longer desire to interact with society.

## FRUSTRATION CAN LEAD TO DEPRESSION

Although frustration is covered thoroughly in Chapter Eight it is mentioned briefly here because it is another operation of the mind that can lead to depression. ***Frustration*** is **an erroneous interpretation of life's experiences.** It brings all movement, naturally and spiritually, to a halt. When you cannot see situations, circumstances and relationships the way God sees them, you will produce erroneous conclusions in your mind about the position of things in your surroundings. Frustration is discontentment, caused by either a lack of exposure to the truth, or a rejection of the truth to which you were exposed.

Frustration can lead one into great distress. ***Distress*** is **narrowness of thought, or to categorize events in circumstances or relationships as calamitous beyond solution.** It causes you to become small in your thinking and thus you have to suppress reasoning, counsel and hope.

## STRESS CAN ALSO BE AN AGENT OF DEPRESSION

***Stress*** means **to over-extend the workings of the mind; to involve it in too many projects.** Therefore, true expression of emotions, thoughts or ideas concerning either project is not allowed. Each project has its own set of circumstances, situations and relationships to which the mind feels obligated to respond. However, the multitude of projects, produce a subtle urgency for mental response to each. The rapidity of response to all the scenarios can cause the mind to be over-extended and fatigued. This is also caused by feelings or ideas being put on hold for one project while another is being dealt with. Here again is suppression of emotions and thoughts, which lead to depression.

## DOUBT

Doubt is another operation of the mind that can lead one into depression. **Doubt** means **not accepting the Word of God as truth.** It holds an element of truth, but wavers over to unbelief or a lack of acceptance of that truth. Doubt is never sure of the end. It can only half-heartedly hope for good to prevail. Doubt cannot trust God or anyone else totally. Therefore, it cannot truly love freely or godly. Emotions are suppressed and joy is lost in uncertainty. The only deliverance is to accept and trust the Word of God as the final authority in every situation, circumstance and relationship.

## AN UNFORGIVING HEART

Forgiveness has proven to be a hard task for many saints. This should not be the case. After all, God was gracious and loving enough to forgive our trespasses against Him. I think many Christians are still unaware of the negative ramifications they will encounter as a result of their refusal to forgive those who offend them.

**Unforgiveness causes you to override your conscence and the Holy Ghost in order to keep hurts, disappointments and pain alive.** Love is suppressed and therefore all emotions and liberating thoughts are depressed. This hardness of the heart forbids the expression of true love, kindness, affection and consideration of another. Again, you must accept the Word of God as the final authority and be willing to allow it to heal you. Consider the following scripture.

**Proverbs 16:6**
> *By mercy and truth, iniquity is purged: and by the fear of the Lord men depart from evil.*

## SUPPRESSION

**When the heart faints, all emotions, thoughts and desires are confined to the imagination**. The imagination is the burial ground. None of these seem able to be expressed in the flesh. Therefore, they are buried deep enough so that the flesh no longer feels deprived. This burial also serves as a protective device from the pain that accompanies suppression. If the burial is deep enough, these emotions and thoughts will seemingly cease to exist. This learned behavior becomes readily accepted, because it is the ultimate cover-up.

Although suppressed, these emotions, thoughts and desires still exist. However, they continue to desire an outlet for expression. You may not even be aware of this. You may be deceived by satan's perfect mask. He will use this scenario to convince you that the mindset developed is actually your true character. You will believe this if you have no teaching to the contrary.

**The emotions that are common to suppression are: <u>anger</u>, <u>wrath</u>, <u>hurt</u> and <u>disappointment</u>**. These feelings are internalized as the mind must protect itself from exposure and deliver itself from hurt and disappointment. The true disposition is therefore buried deep inside the imagination of the heart. The soil there will be fertile, if the Word of God is not hidden in the heart. This lying mindset, with its lying emotions, is used as a burial garment for your true feelings. But as is the case with all fleshy things, the covering will eventually rot and the seed of all the hurt, anger, disappointment and wrath will take root in the heart.

## THE HEART KNOWS ITS OWN BITTERNESS

This root is one of *bitterness* (resulting from or expressive of severe grief, anguish, or disappointment; strong animosity). King Solomon really understood this false disposition of the fleshy mind. Let us take a look at some of his writings from the book of Proverbs.

**Proverbs 14:10**
> *<u>The heart knoweth his own bitterness;</u> and a stranger doth not intermeddle with his joy.*

**Proverbs 14:13**

*Even in laughter the heart is sorrowful; and the end of that mirth is heaviness.*

**Proverbs 15:13**

*A merry heart maketh a cheerful countenance: but by sorrow of heart is the spirit broken.*

The heart knows its own bitterness. It has experienced, entertained and nurtured it deep in the darkness of the imagination. Even though the face wears a smile and the overall attitude is one of contentment, there is sorrow on the inside. The end is going to be heaviness, which is the Biblical term for sorrow or grief.

The spirit or exhalation of the soul will be broken, as the root continues to grow, consuming all righteous desires and peace. The will becomes paralyzed and is unable to fight back. The absence of the Word of God in your heart will make it easy for a root of bitterness to strangle every good and pleasant thing in the soul. This root of bitterness will affect the inward parts in such a way that it will be reflected in your overall character. It will cause your belief system to change. In the end, there will be an acceptance of a new mindset of hopelessness, because the flesh still has not provided an outlet for the expression of the original feelings and thoughts. The mind will seek to protect itself by turning against the flesh and labeling it as the enemy.

# A TRANSIC OR PLATONIC STATE OF MIND

Although interactions with those in your sphere of influence may be restrained, the heart knows its own bitterness. It lives on in the world of the imagination, separate and apart from the activities of the flesh. This mental state could progress into either a <u>transic</u> or <u>platonic</u> state of mind.

***Transic*** means to be completely lost in thought or meditation as to be unaware of one's surroundings.

A person in a ***platonic state of mind*** is usually very legalistic and void of any affection or outward show of emotion. *(The definitions for Platonic and Transic were formed or derived from divine study, revelations and Webster's Dictionary).*

If something happens to challenge the authenticity of the displayed mindset, such as the invasion of truth, the mind must then fight to keep the covering secure. Likewise, if something inside a relationship is done to awaken the desire to truly express emotions and thoughts of the heart, the mind will either surrender to the desire or withdraw even further into darkness.

As I said earlier, we must see every situation through the eyes of God. <u>Depression is an act of withdrawal from a present reality into a world of grayed horizons and shadows of figures.</u> This is a world where there is no structure and the light of it becomes dimmer each day. This is a world I am quite familiar because at a very young age, I sank into that horrible abyss called depression.

Tanya is with her father for the summer and Michael and Michelle are with their Grandmother. But where was I? This room is not familiar to me. It is small and the mattress on the pull-out bed seems damp. The clock on the microwave says 6:13...is it that late already? I need to go make some phone calls. I saw a few jobs in the paper. I think I'll take a shower and go down to the park just to get out of the house. I need to finish reading that chapter in Isaiah. If I had a car I could go up to Palm Beach and see Mama. I can't believe I slept all day. Now you know you've been sleeping all day every day for quite a while now. Get up Mary and do something. Go see Gloria. See what she's up to. Yeah, but then what? We'll laugh and talk for awhile but Gloria doesn't really know me. She doesn't know what I really want to do. She probably wouldn't believe it anyway. What is that on the wall? It looks like someone started to carve their name or something. I forgot to wash out that white blouse today. Oh Lord, I'm about to miss his show. I hope he finishes that lesson he was teaching last week. Let me get my notes. What kind of work can I do to make some quick money? Michael is going to be a preacher. I know he is. I need to get a place and go get all my children. Tanya might not want to come back home. Things have been pretty rough here. She can't take this. Besides, she hates me for not keeping a job like I used to. The house is gone; and that little money I got from it is gone too. This bed is so hard. It's dark outside. I better lay back down.

Beloved, this was my mind continuously, day after day. Every thought was a dead-end. Words like "go" and "get up" revealed the weight of a millstone tied to my waste. I can't go. Go where? There was nothing in the world outside for me. There was no continuity in my thinking; therefore, I could not focus. I studied the Word daily, but God was not using me either. I had no direction. I didn't know what to do. I had no confidence in any potential project. I was a preacher with no place to preach. I was living holy; I had truly repented of my sin. Yet God didn't even seem to want me in His service.

It wasn't supposed to be like this. I gave up all my businesses and any professional aspirations to be free to preach the gospel. But there was no one there to teach, train, or even prepare me for the pitfalls of full-time evangelism. I knew nothing about starting a ministry. People had started calling me to preach in their churches and I thought this is surely the launching of my ministerial career.

Where were the elders? Where were the wise men and women who nurtured and spiritually developed young saplings like myself? Why didn't they rush upon me and tell me I wasn't ready for what the devil was bringing my way? He was tall, dark and handsome; gifted and charismatic. He was a one-man church. He could sing, dance, preach and pray. We seemed to fit like a pair of leather gloves. We both fell prey to the deception of sin.

But one day, I realized my love for God and ministry was greater than anything I could experience in this world. I walked away and went to seek my God. I begged and pleaded for forgiveness. I was horrified by the thought of not being able to serve the Lord.

Had my prayers been answered? Yes, God had forgiven me for the sin. This I know, because He really and truly strengthened me with a spirit of might in my inner man. I was able to walk away and stay away. Repentance and submission to the righteousness of God had removed any desire to renew the relationship.

I thank God for the prayers of the righteous saints who prayed for me. Though the darkness was so great and all consuming, I had to find a way to focus on the truth in order to come back to reality. I had to repent for allowing any distractions to my purpose. If you find yourself slipping into depression, cry out to the Lord before it is too late or before you fall so far that you forget the power of your own prayers.

**The second alternative for the mind is to accept, as reality, the cruel rejection of its attempts to express its innermost feelings.** The unfair response of loved ones or authoritative figures must be dealt with. The only way to deal with this truth, without the presence of the Word of God, is to fight back with hatred, strife and malice. These destructive feelings are good protection and cover-up devices used to conceal true feelings of love and affection.

Once again, true nature, thoughts, ideas and character are suppressed, while rebellion and hatred rule the relationship. Consequently, one does not have to appear physically depressed to be withdrawn from expression of true emotion. Men and women alike suffer from this depressed state of mind. Some men cover it with abuse or meanness, lack of sensitivity or hardness of heart. Women on the other hand, being accustomed to living out of their emotions, will respond with what appears to be outright hatred and vindictiveness. In either case, love, affection and kindness is withdrawn from their relationships, as a form of punishment to those whom they have become fearful to love and trust.

This does not mean they do not want to love others. They have been deprived; therefore, no one else deserves to receive that which they have not received. Nevertheless, the root of bitterness grows and the poison spreads. Their character may become one of meanness and hatefulness. This is sad because children, husbands and wives alike suffer in this situation.

Can this mindset be changed? Yes, it can be changed.
1. You must accept the truth and see yourself as who you really are.
2. You must try to understand how you got to where you are.
3. You must be willing to accept the Word of God, not people, as the healing balm.
4. You must also be willing to be re-educated as to how to allow love and kindness to flow from your heart into the lives of others.

You can choose to accept the fact that your feelings and emotions have been suppressed throughout childhood, but become determined to overcome this reality with a new mindset. You can purpose in your heart not to allow yourself to remain depressed due to suppressed feelings and thoughts. You can agree with God. The old man is dead with all his hurts, timidity, obsessions and frustrations. You are new. The life you live in the flesh now is Christ. He is not depressed or suppressed. He always trusts and agrees with the Father.

**The Word of God will deliver you.** The Word can destroy the effects of the offenses to your emotions and restore the God-given right to communicate. Strive to be sober. Accept the fact that your mind was suppressed, worked or driven into depression. All this may be true, but God has given you the answer. You can win this battle. You are worth it. Fight to speak your true heart. The Word will teach you how to speak your true feelings without offending others.

The Word will open up a completely new world of emotions and desires. It will build courage in your heart so that the habit of suppression will be broken. It will teach you how to walk in the Spirit of God. If you are not sitting in a church that has a revelation of the Christ in you, then ask the Father to lead you to one that does. It is the knowledge of Christ that strengthens us in our inner man. Do not lie to yourself. If you suffer from these captivities of the mind, then seek out the riches of God's glory for deliverance. Do not withdraw and do not push forward into pride, but stand fast and allow the liberty of Christ to make you free.

# OVERCOMING POLITICAL FEARS

The political unrest in this country has opened the door for spirits of hatred and violence. Sad to say, many Christians are guilty of such. Oh no, they are not possessed (those who are truly born-again that is), but their own spirits are full of hatred and violence. These are people who claim to have a moral and righteous obligation to contend for Christian values. But when they lose at the polls they throw the Bible in the trash along with other virtues such as love, temperance, contentment and faith.

John was a very hard working man, a loving husband and father. He was a very good provider for his family. He served as a deacon in his church and even coached a little league baseball team. His children adored him and his wife was very happy. The home was full of love and laughter. But suddenly John's routine changed. Instead of coming directly home after work, every Friday John (who never drank before), would stop at the bar and liquor store on the way home to have a few drinks with the boys and to pick up a bottle of his favorite brew. Though he never was a fall-down drunk, by the time John got home, he was quite high and feeling no pain, as they say. His wife would have the house spotless, the table set and the children would be extremely quiet.

Nervously, they would sit at the table, afraid to say anything. They did not speak unless spoken to by their father.

This was learned behavior they had adopted in order to get through Friday nights. Things would be different and back to normal by Saturday morning. John would become bad-tempered and mean while under the influence of alcohol. He would nitpick; always finding something to complain about. He would yell at the kids and curse at his wife. Nothing was satisfactory anymore. From Friday evening to Saturday morning the mood of the house would be that of fear and terror. The next day, John would be completely sober and back to his gentle, loving, kind self.

In most cases, a liquor store displays the sign, **Wine and Spirits**. The ability of alcohol to break down one's will and to release pent-up hostilities and rage is powerful. While under the influence, John would become a different personality. His spirit would change and he did things he would have never done while sober. The influence of the alcohol on the soul caused John to forget or cast aside all the values he lived by.

The same is true of the church. The issues of our times are affecting our nation adversely. More and more hostilities are heating up over candidates, policies and the moral decay of our society. The American dream is fading and tempers are rising. But just as John allowed the influence of alcohol to change his spirit, even so have many Christians allowed the issues of our times to change their spiritual disposition. This is true even in light of the fact Jesus said, *"...In the world ye shall have tribulation: but be of good cheer, I have overcome the world" (St. John 16:33).* Even in casual conversation, the negative disposition of the heart can be heard; *for out of the abundance of the heart the mouth speaketh (Matthew 12:34).*

For example, I have had the privilege of working with many born-again believers who are very passionate about politics. These are very good people, who really love the Lord and cherish moral and Christian values. However, I have discovered you cannot discuss politics with them because it would always manifest their walk after the flesh. You can really hear their negative spiritual disposition when discussing certain political leaders. You can sense a deep-rooted spirit of hatred when politics is mentioned.

This is an excellent example of God allowing conversation to reveal where a person is spiritually. Even Gabriel reframed from launching a wailing accusation against satan, as he disputed over the body of Moses. However, many Christians have ceased to discern the spirit they respond in when their livelihood is threatened. If you cannot talk about the leaders of your nation with love and mercy, then it manifests that you harbor iniquity in your heart. These are the people God instructed us to pray for. But how can you pray for someone you hate? *If I regard iniquity in my heart, the Lord will not hear me (Psalm 66:18).* The hatred of government has permeated the Church, and Christians will not deal with that truth.

The hatred spewed out towards the present American government (2014) has totally taken away many saints' ability to pray effectual fervent prayers. God is not listening to them. That is a truth they refuse to accept. They all go through the motions; joining prayer groups and spiritual watches that are supposed to be sending up prayers to the Father on behalf of their nation. These prayers never leave the earth. They simply fall to the ground. But I can hear a voice echoing from heaven, "Oh, if I only had an intercessor. Surely, I would heal their land."

We walk in disobedience because we do not regard scripture and therefore, become conformed to this world. We put our hope in government officials; many who do not even know God. The scripture declares we are not to be entangled with the affairs of this world (2 Timothy 2:4). If we say that our trust is in God, why do we worry about who is leading the nation? Your livelihood does not depend on who is in political office. We must remember that all things work together for good to them that love God (Romans 8:28). Everything that God does is done with His people in mind. He is our Father. The government is not in control; God is.

## Romans 13:1

*Let every soul be subject unto the higher powers. For there is no power but of God: the powers that be are ordained of God.*

We must submit to the head of our government, even if he is wrong on some political issues. The scriptures declare Jesus even submitted to government officials. When it came time to pay taxes, He sent Peter to catch a fish and in its mouth was enough money to pay their taxes. Jesus stepped out of heaven and became subject to an evil Roman government. Even if oour government doesn't deserve our benevolence, we must give it anyway.

The fear of losing materialistic things should not be named among the saints. Our trust should be in our God. We must be content in whatever state the Lord allows us to be in. *Servants, be subject to your masters with all fear; not only to the good and gentle, but also to the froward (1 Peter 2:18).*

Although things are happening in our government that are causing us to lose houses, jobs, etc., we, as Sons of God, are instructed to submit to those who are set as higher powers; and pray for them. If we can pray for those who offend us, we then qualify to pray for our loved ones.

Furthermore, why do those who are in the Body of Christ become so frantic about what is happening in the world? Our Kingdom is not of this world. We are citizens of the Kingdom of God. We have been instructed not to love the world, neither the things that are in this world. Our only reason for being here is to bring others into the Kingdom. We are in this world; but we are not of this world.

Even though Romans 13:1 declares the powers that be are approved of God, the Body of Christ doesn't believe this. It believes men appointed our elected officials. If we believed these powers were ordained by God, perhaps we would not have a problem submitting to what God has set before us; seeking Him for the answer as to how to exist in this hostile environment He has allowed to be created.

## Romans 13:2
*Whosoever therefore resisteth the power, resisteth*

*the ordinance of God: and they that resist shall receive to themselves damnation.*

**Damnation** is the **loosening of the destroyer in your life; the end result of which could be eternal damnation (hell).** When we speak evil of the power and ordinations of God, we open the door for the enemy to bring damnation into our territorial sphere of influence. In addition, it hinders prayer, our well-being and ministry. Remember, the enemy comes to kill, steal and destroy.

**Romans 13:3**
> *For rulers are not a terror to good works, but to the evil. Wilt thou then not be afraid of the power? do that which is good, and thou shalt have praise of the same.*

The state of the nation should not be a terror to the sons of God. If the government spends all the money in the national budget, it should not be a terror to us. Our treasures are in heaven. The big issue today is money; all of it is being spent. The scriptures declare that mammon is another god, and we cannot serve it and Christ. We should not have the same mindset as the world concerning this matter.

We must reverence God for the things He allows in the earth. He is the power behind all rulers. He holds their lives in His hand. We, the saints of God act as if God is impotent and powerless in the political arena. But the Word of God declared in ancient times, Daniel counseled King Nebuchadnezzar on this wise: *Thy kingdom shall be sure unto thee, after that thou shalt have known that the heavens do rule (Daniel 4:26).*

After seven years of chastening, the king came to his right mind again and declared…*all the inhabitants of the earth are reputed as nothing: and he doeth according to his will in the army of heaven, and among the inhabitants of the earth: and none can stay his hand, or say unto him, What doest thou? (Daniel 4:35).*

## Romans 13:4

> ***For he is the minister of God to thee for good. But if thou do that which is evil, be afraid; for he beareth not the sword in vain: for he is the minister of God, a revenger to execute wrath upon him that doeth evil.***

The higher powers that be are ministers of God for the good of His people. Remember, all things work together for good to them that love God; and to them who are called according to His purpose. God is the One who puts in the hearts of men the things He wants carried out in the earth. Laws which are placed in the books, as well as those that are not passed are all orchestrated by God. Our leaders are men and women being used to carry out His will. Whether good or bad, all things are done for the good of God's people. These scriptures reveal how much we exalt flesh, and disregard God and His Word.

If the sword that is placed in the minister's hand is not in vain, then it stands to reason that whatever he destroys was in the plan of God for our sake. The Roman Government was the cruelest government that ever ruled the world; and one that ruled the longest. They were so cruel God styled them as a beast with teeth of iron. According to Romans 13:4, they were the ministers of God. He allowed the Caesars to kill His people. God allowed little Christian children to be sown up in animal skins, soaked in blood and fed to bears. He allowed Nero to use Christians as human torches to light up his garden so that he might see how to eat. God placed the sword in his hand.

## WHAT ABOUT THE CANDIDATES THEMSELVES?

We must learn how to discern the spiritual connotation of everything and compare spiritual with spiritual. Everything we see in the natural must also be seen through the eyes of the Spirit; even politics.

There are some candidates who run for office confessing to be born-again, but will stand on a platform and deliberately say things that will incite violence, simply because they were instructed to do so. What happened to the morals they campaigned for? In the face of getting elected, anything goes. It's just like John mentioned in the scenario at the beginning of this chapter, "When the campaign is over, I'll go back to my Christian virtues." Whether candidate or voter, we must stay within the boundaries of the faith; even in politics.

The death of Osama Ben Laden is a testimony to how Christians have departed from trusting in the true and living God, to trusting in the actions of humanity. There were many Christians who joined in the celebration of Ben

Laden's death. They paraded and danced in the streets, right along with those who do not know God.

The fall of Wall Street and the continuous decline in our global economic status is a reality we never considered possible. Ben Laden and his terrorist groups not only threatened our American way of life, but also proved he could indeed change it. The greatest manifestation of this change is the "fear factor." America is a nation that was hurled into a chasm of fear, likened unto that which other nations have experienced for years. But what are the spiritual connotations here? Wherein is the power of Christianity? After all, we claim to be the most Christian nation in the world. But the "fear of loss," whether it is life, limb, or property, has caused the true character of the saints to come forth. Could it be the Father has allowed such events, that it might manifest the distance the church has fallen away from the true heart and mind of God.

The church rejoiced fervently at the death of Ben Laden. At that moment he ceased to be a soul in need of a Savior, he was just another threat to our life-style that had been eliminated.

If you do not trust God, you will think and do that which is evil. If you want to get God to move on your behalf, learn how to trust Him. Don't ever lose faith in God. When you put your faith in anything other than God, you mock Him. Money did not bring us to where we are now; our peace is not found in the material things of this world. Our hope is not in politicians, elected officials, or 'special forces' units. They do not establish our goings nor are they able to secure our wellbeing.

In order to overcome the fear of the politics of our time, you must first come into agreement with God. Admit where you are and the way you think. The truth you must accept is that:

(1) You suffer from a lack of contentment in God.
(2) You are offended by God's control of your life and the things that affect it.
(3) Your heart is full of iniquity towards some of the men and women He has placed in power.

Beloved, just admit where you are. Confess the sins of your heart and take the counsel of the script.... *let us cleanse ourselves from all filthiness of the flesh and spirit, perfecting holiness in the fear of God (2 Corinthians 7:1).* If you do not get rid of the iniquity, it will destroy you. It will keep you separated from God and man. It is torment worse than the fear you carry. Fight to maintain a pure heart in all things. Again, the scripture instructs us saying, *if we live in the Spirit, let us also walk in the Spirit (Galatians 5:25).*

God is shaking up His Church. He is allowing many things to happen to show forth the saints who will stand regardless of what's happening with the government. He is bringing to the forefront those who trust Him. There is a true changing of the guard taking place right now; and the spirits of just men are taking their places in leadership. They have the ear of the Father and are echoing the voice of the Chief Shepherd. His sheep will know His voice, and another they will not follow. He is identifying the real Church. Not all who say, "Lord, Lord," are a part of that glorious assembly.

I know that we have come to a time when truth will be exalted. God has raised up those of us who are willing to preach the real gospel of Jesus Christ at any cost. Having worked with many different nationalities and socio-economic groups, it has been made clear to me that many of those who are given an opportunity to hear these truths will not embrace them. Fascinatingly, many will rally to hear and rejoice that they are made privy to such knowledge, but when the bottom line is reached, they will not give their heart over to the truth they will have heard.

I have had first-hand experience among those who fit the above criteria. I am amazed at how they admit to the truth, testify of its authenticity, yet in the next hour challenge it with doctrines or fruitless church activities they already know to be heretic in nature and powerless in their ability to produce the character of Christ. I have never seen anything like this. When truth bears witness with our spirit and is confirmed by the Holy Ghost in us, wherein is the fight? Better still, why is the fight necessary? I think I would understand if the truth I speak of was something these people did not readily understand. That is not the case. They do not understand truth and the witness of the Spirit they applaud and then reject.

**2 Timothy 3:1-9**
*1 This know also, that in the last days perilous times*

*shall come.*

*2 For men shall be lovers of their own selves, covetous, boasters, proud, blasphemers, disobedient to parents, unthankful, unholy,*

*3 Without natural affection, trucebreakers, false accusers, incontinent, fierce, despisers of those that are good,* (the Greek word used here means; to be hostile to virtue.)

*4 Traitors, heady,* (headstrong) *highminded,* (proud or to be lifted up in pride) *lovers of pleasures more than lovers of God;*

*5 Having a form* (an appearance) *of godliness,* (holiness) *but denying* (to reject) *the power thereof: from such turn away.* The instruction is clear right here. We are warned to turn away from those who resist truth. The Lords knows this resistance is infectious. Therefore, we are encouraged to separate ourselves from those who would seek to negate that which we have received spiritual affirmation of.

*6 For of this sort are they which creep into houses, and lead captive silly women laden with sins, led away with divers lusts,* (be certain here that this creeping can be done on the telephone, or in the church parking lot, or wherever, a conversation is rendered that is designed to steal the affect of truth in the inward parts.

*7 Ever learning, and never able to come to the knowledge of the truth.* These people never allow themselves to experience the power of the truth and work diligently to hinder others in their quest to know the true and living God.

*8 Now as Jannes and Jambres withstood Moses,*

*so do these also resist the truth: men of corrupt minds, reprobate concerning the faith.* It is here we see a foregoing principle; God never changes. He is the same today as He was yesterday. Those who continuously resist the truth risk becoming a castaway, rejected by God and counted as worthless to the faith.

*9 But they shall proceed no further: for their folly shall be manifest unto all men, as theirs also was.* Those who resist His word today will meet with the same fate as those who resisted the word He spoke to Moses. Jannes and Jambres found themselves falling into the pits of hell, as will all who resist the truth given today.

Some time ago, the Lord said to me, "Truth is sufficient." He brought this back to me recently in my dealings with this issue. Discern the intent of the Master here. Open your spirit and really hear what the Spirit is saying. If truth is indeed sufficient, then nothing else added or depleted from it will produce a manifested son of God. This further means God is satisfied with presenting the truth to us. Beyond that, He is finished. In other words, the fail-safe mechanism built into the truth is its ability to quicken or bear witness with our spirit. God designed it that way. Once this is done, the burden is no longer on the Father. It is our responsibility not only to embrace and cherish that truth, but to make it law for our lives. God is finished. That is to say, He is now able to judge those who think to chide with Him by challenging His Word.

# DEALING WITH OFFENSES AND UNFORGIVENESS

This lesson will teach you how to deliver yourself, and others, from the captivity of offenses and unforgiveness that have held so many in bondage for many years.

For as long as we can remember, we have held grudges against those we live with, work for, associate with and love. We console ourselves by giving the "silent treatment," "backbiting," "spreading rumors," or just plain "getting even."

When asked how many times we should forgive our brother who sins against us, Jesus told Peter, "...until seventy times seven" (Matthew 18:22).

This seems an inconceivable task for some, and simply impossible for others. Yet, if our sincere desire is to walk in the character of Christ, we must take on this mindset.

## OFFENSES

An *offense* is **a stumbling block. It is that thing that brings about an occasion to stumble or fall**. An offense can hinder and even stop the flow of love if it is not forgiven. Take time to read the scriptures below for they speak the mind of the Father concerning offenses in the Body of Christ.

## Matthew 6:12, 14-15

*12 And forgive us our debts, as we forgive our debtors*

*14 For if ye forgive men their trespasses, your heavenly Father will also forgive you.*
*15 But if ye forgive not men their trespasses, neither will your Father forgive your trespasses.*

## Luke 17:1-10

*1 Then said he unto the disciples, It is impossible but that offenses will come: but woe unto him, through whom they come!*
*2 It were better for him that a millstone were hanged about his neck, and he cast into the sea, than that he should offend one of these little ones.*
*3 Take heed to yourselves: If thy brother trespass against thee, rebuke him; and if he repent, forgive him.*
*4 And if he trespass against thee seven times in a day, and seven times in a day turn again to thee, saying, I repent; thou shalt forgive him.*
*5 And the apostles said unto the Lord, Increase our faith.*
*6 And the Lord said, If ye had faith as a grain of mustard seed, ye might say unto this sycamine tree, Be thou plucked up by the root, and be thou planted in the sea; and it should obey you.*
*7 But which of you, having a servant plowing*

*or feeding cattle, will say unto him by and*
*by, when he is come from the field, Go and*
*sit down to meat?*
*8 And will not rather say unto him, Make*
*ready wherewith I may sup, and gird thyself,*
*and serve me, till I have eaten and drunken;*
*and afterward thou shalt eat and drink?*
*9 Doth he thank that servant because he did*
*the things that were commanded him?   I*
*trow not.*
*10 So likewise ye, when ye shall have done*
*all those things which are commanded you,*
*say, We are unprofitable servants:  we have*
*done that which was our duty to do.*

The Lord admonishes us that offenses will come; even though He puts a woe upon the one who brings the offense. However, the woe will come from the Lord, not from us. There will be those who will sin against us maliciously, but the Lord instructs us to forgive each offense.

When Jesus insisted that the apostles were to forgive as many as seven offenses in the run of a day, the apostles began to question their ability to do such a thing. Consequently, they asked the Lord to increase their faith. Many times we think of having "great faith" only as a necessity to perform great healings or miracles. **However, the first work of faith is to prepare the heart to love the way God loves.**

Notice also that Jesus acknowledged that they did not have the kind of faith He knew was necessary to extend this kind of love to their fellowman. They were only considering belief as the definition of faith. **Jesus came to introduce a Dispensation of Faith, which is the Operation of the Holy Ghost in the lives of the sons of God.** This dispensational Faith (the indwelling of the Holy Ghost) would be more powerful than that of mere belief. It would be functional. It would be effectual. It would bring the believer to a place of perfection, wherein he loves his God with all his heart and his fellow man as himself. This faith would be the fulfilling of all the commandments.

## THE SYCAMINE TREE

Notice too, that Jesus symbolized the most painful of all offenses as a sycamine tree. The sycamine tree is a type of mulberry tree. The thing that distinguishes it from the other trees in its family is its <u>black</u> fruit. The analogy is that the fruit of an offense left to grow inside of the sons of God is black . . . very black. Take note, Jesus declares that the operation of the Holy Ghost in the life of the believer is powerful enough to pluck even such a thing up by the roots.

Offenses must be disposed of at the root. There must not be a trace of the root left. If the root is left, the tree will grow again ... *lest any root of bitterness springing up trouble you, and thereby many be defiled (Hebrews 12:15).*

Paul insists that roots of bitterness springing up from offenses will trouble you and defile others. But what does he mean when he says, "trouble you?" Quite simply, it means that <u>bitterness will rob you of your ability to love.</u> It will indeed stop the flow of love. Remember, for the sons of God, the desire to love is innate; therefore, **you will be uncomfortable not being able to love your brother or sister**. You will have to entertain certain foreign, yet painful emotions every time that individual is mentioned, or the thought of the offense is brought to mind. This is not normal, and the stress placed on fleshy emotions will cripple your will and darken your imagination.

But Paul does not stop there. He insists that <u>your bitterness will defile others</u>. What others? He is referring to those who are involved in relationships with you. It will rob them of experiencing your love. It will also hinder them in their attempt to love you. Therefore, if those in your relationships do not experience your love, it is because they have become victims of your iniquity.

It is erroneous to think that your hatred of another does not affect those whom you believe you love. Your loved ones have to live with the iniquity you have for others. They are often made weary by your disposition with others. They can never look to you for spiritual support, because they know that your heart is not pure and free from iniquity.

Furthermore, it is erroneous to think that you can love only certain people. If you are one to hold offenses against those outside your marriage or immediate family, you will do the same to those in the immediate family and to your spouse. A rattlesnake is a rattlesnake. It does not care who it bites. If you will not forgive your sister, you will not forgive your spouse, if he or she commits the offense that tests your love.

Nevertheless, Jesus declared that Faith (the operation of the Holy Ghost) is capable of plucking up monumental iniquity by the roots.

## BREAKING FREE OF OFFENSES

The term ***unforgiveness*** means **to hold in the heart the sin and trespasses of another**. It burdens that person with guilt and condemnation. It stops the flow of love, leaving no possibility of reconciliation until unforgiveness is destroyed.

The root of unforgiveness is bitterness from what the fleshy mind and the emotions interpret as an offense. You can receive counsel, go to the altar, talk to God and still have unforgiveness lodged in your heart.

Unforgiveness must be purged out of the heart. This purging must be from the inside out. Just because you discuss an offense does not mean you are healed. You must overcome the offense. The word ***overcome*** means to **overtake.** In other words, you must overcome it with something more powerful than the offense itself. And there is only one thing that is more powerful than offenses. LOVE. Only the love of God that flows from us like rivers of living water will destroy the power of an offense.

## OVERCOMING INIQUITY

**Ephesians 4:26-27, 29-32**
*26 Be ye angry, and sin not: let not the sun go down upon your wrath:*

*27 Neither give place to the devil . . .*

*29 Let no corrupt communication proceed out of your mouth, but that which is good to the use of edifying, that it may minister grace unto the hearers.*

*30 And grieve not the holy Spirit of God, whereby ye are sealed unto the day of redemption.*

*31 Let all bitterness, and wrath, and anger, and clamour, and evil speaking, be put away from you, with all malice:*

*32 And be ye kind one to another, tenderhearted, forgiving one another, even as God for Christ's sake hath forgiven you.*

Notice that to carry the offense for even a day is an occasion to sin. It is a time for iniquity to develop in the heart. When you disobey this commandment, you give a place in your heart to the devil. Then, He can install his devices in your imagination. Consider also that the scripture admonished you to go to your sister or brother if you have an ought with one.

## Matthew 18:15

*Moreover if thy brother shall trespass against thee, go and tell him his fault between thee and him alone: if he shall hear thee, thou hast gained thy brother.*

If there is contention between you and someone else, go to them with a heart that seeks reconciliation. This "going to" was designed to stop the development of iniquity, not to purge iniquity that has already developed. Your purpose in going must be to keep iniquity from forming in your heart. However, after iniquity is formed, going to your brother may not remove the iniquity.

Remember the offense is in you. It has already taken root, and formed iniquity in your heart. However, you must realize your spiritual location is not dependent upon how people treat you. In fact, if the offense has already formed iniquity in your heart, then going to the other person with iniquity in your heart could possibly make the situation worse. The ability to purge the heart of iniquity has nothing to do with the other person. It is an act of absolute obedience to the will of the Father.

## INIQUITY WILL CHANGE YOUR PERSONALITY

When you do not deal righteously with offenses, iniquity grows and begins to consume you. The manifestation of this is in the shaping of your personality. The way you deal with people now will be determined by how you have dealt with offenses of your past. If you were unsuccessful in dealing with those offenses, you will certainly handle present day circumstances and relationships in remembrance of the hurts and pain of yesterday. Others will suffer because of your past hurts. <u>Others will be denied the beauty of real love from you because of your nurtured pain from the past</u>.

**The truth is the personality others experience is not the real you.** The real you is buried in the pain and crucified in the hurts. The real you wants to love and trust again, but the risk seems to be too great. You are afraid of hurting and trusting again. You are afraid of feeling the same pain.

The truth is you are already hurting without trusting. You are already hurting without loving. You are miserable.

Whenever you refuse to deal with offenses in righteousness, iniquity is bred. You can lose confidence in your own spirituality, because you continue to "not" do the righteous thing. Your "will to do" can be broken. When your will to deal righteously is broken, you will experience spiritual depression (which is the opposite of spiritual stress).

**Spiritual stress results when we force the fleshy mind and the body to do the righteous thing, without wholehearted agreement in the soul.**

**Spiritual depression comes from the knowledge that you are not dealing righteously.**

The devil wants to <u>justify</u> your position by saying it would not do you any good to do the righteous thing. Believing this lie strengthens the depression.

There is a way out of this prison. You can deliver yourself from the pain of the past. How? By dealing with the offenses of today. Remember, iniquity must be purged out of the heart. **It must be overcome by something more powerful.** Target a present situation. Determine to change the way you internally deal with the offense. You can absorb the present offense by doing the righteous thing. You must deal with offenses the way the Word instructs.

**When you do the righteous thing, old hatred and bitterness will be purged.** When you operate in love, this digs out any residue of negative fleshy emotions. If you deal in righteousness with present offenses, it will purge you of the pain you once suffered from old offenses. When you walk in love, you see old offenders differently. Because you are walking in the Spirit, your mind is renewed; and because the iniquity that shaped your personality is purged, your personality will change. Love is more powerful than iniquity.

Too often we hide behind religious foolishness. What happens if the other person refuses to reconcile, or continues to feel the same about you? The enemy will make you feel you are not delivered because someone does not say what you want to hear.

**The iniquity of bitterness is a spiritual flaw.** Do not allow the devil to discourage you. Your deliverance is not based upon someone agreeing with or apologizing to you. The Word of God delivers. You must meet and overcome evil with good. Go now and find an adverse object to love. Seek out someone to love who has really done you wrong. Prove the **power** of love and obedience to God.

**Again, deal with the present day offenses and offenders.** (The offender may or may not be someone who offended you in the past.) You must deal with friends who are hurting you now. Allowing love to flow today will purge you of the hurts of the past. Please understand that distrusting people because of offenses does not stop there. It filters over into your relationship with God. It is impossible for someone operating in this disposition to trust God. Your mind has been trained not to trust or believe in love. If you do not trust God, you will not trust His Word.

## VULNERABILITY: A STEP TOWARD DELIVERANCE

How do you get back to trusting God? You must make yourself vulnerable. Look upon your offender with pity, and see them as a soul. The offense is then absorbed. The most they can do is vex your spirit. When love flows, it opens the floodgates and the spiritual enemies of your past are drowned in the sea of forgetfulness.

Remember, once iniquity has set in, the evil has progressed. Talking will not remove the spiritual disposition. Once iniquity is established, you must get rid of it with love. If you go to a past offender, with the wrong motive, you may end up worse than you were before you went. The offender may lay another offense in your life. We are responsible for delivering ourselves from the snare. If you harbor iniquity in your heart, you can be used by the devil. Your iniquity will become his stronghold.

If you want to purge yourself of iniquity, then you must not avoid your offenders, but instead, seek them out with love and allow patience to have her perfect work. God is depending on you to reveal the power that is in the gospel of Jesus Christ.

**The ministry of reconciliation does not lay the offense to the offender's charge.** You must deal with the offender without holding him or her responsible. You judge. Which is more profitable? To hold on to the hatred, or to get rid of it and God be glorified?

# THE TRANSFORMATION

If you have gotten this far in reading this book, then it is obvious you are seeking a complete revelation, as it relates to your spiritual and even natural state of being. I praise God for you. I trust the Lord will bring clarity and a quenching of your thirst for righteousness.

I have tried desperately to convince you that a sinless life here on earth is possible. I know that this is not a popular view, but it is the one the scriptures proclaim. Even so, in order for me to successfully make my point, I must deal with what seems to be the opposition that negates my knowledge in this mystery.

## The Questions . . .

1. *"If we are created holy and complete in Christ, then why do I still have these desires and emotions that plague my mind daily?"*

2. *"If I have the mind of Christ, then why do I crave the things of the world?"*

Beloved, these are fair and honest questions. You need not be ashamed to have asked them in your heart. The questions themselves speak to the fact that you are uncomfortable with longing for certain things. Your soul hungers and thirsts for the knowledge of God. It is that knowledge that will bring peace, joy and fulfillment in your walk with God.

The answers to these questions are simple. They are not hard. There are many sons of God whose eyes are not single.

**Matthew 6:22-24**
*22 The light of the body is the eye: if therefore thine eye be single, thy whole body shall be full of light.*
*23 But if thine eye be evil, thy whole body shall be full of darkness. If therefore the light that is in thee be darkness, how great is that darkness!*
*24 No man can serve two masters: for either he will hate the one, and love the other; or else he will hold to the one, and despise the other. Ye cannot serve God and mammon.*

Thinking creates desires and feelings. The moment we begin to look into the world for things or pleasures, we forsake the desires of the Spirit. When the soul desires to experience things that are forbidden, it usurps authority over the body and instructs the fleshy mind to think on those things that are unlawful. This wrong thinking creates lust and wantonness in the flesh.

I need you to remember the principles of the previous chapters. I will keep them before you as we continue, for it is of a certainty that all that follows must be built upon the foundation already laid.

1. You have been reborn into the family of God, thus you are the partaker of the divine nature.
2. The body of sin has been destroyed through the circumcision of the flesh.
3. Restoration has come. As Adam was before the fall, you are sanctified; body, soul and spirit. But you are even better than Adam was; you are divine in nature and the enemy cannot live in you again as he lived in Adam. Your body is now the temple of the Holy Ghost.
4. You are a free moral agent. Your slate is clean. You can choose whom you will serve: sin unto death or righteousness unto life eternal.
5. You can grow into the fullness of the stature of the man, Jesus Christ. There are no captivities that can hinder you.
6. You must learn Christ.

These are the facts. You have been made free and clean. But you were born a babe that must grow up into the stature of a man. *But ye have not so learned Christ; If so be that ye have heard him, and have been taught by him, as the truth is in Jesus: That ye put off concerning the former conversation the old man, which is corrupt according to the deceitful lusts; And be renewed in the spirit of your mind; And that ye put on the new man, which after God is created in righteousness and true holiness (Eph 4:20-24).* This in no way implies a lack in anything but knowledge.

A healthy child is born with all its faculties, but he must be taught how to use them. The same is true for the Sons of God. *For when for the time ye ought to be teachers,*

*ye have need that one teach you again which be the first*
*principles of the oracles of God; and are become such as*
*have need of milk, and not of strong meat. For every one*
*that useth milk is unskilful in the word of righteousness:*
*for he is a babe. But strong meat belongeth to them that*
*are of full age,* <u>*even those who by reason of use have their*</u>
<u>*senses exercised to discern both good and evil*</u> *(Heb 5:12-*
*14).*

It is time for the Sons to hear a sure word; one that will
cause them to grow in the knowledge of the power of that
which has apprehended them.

If only we could have heard the truth from the beginning,
and had not been poisoned by mixed manna and false
doctrines that were poured into the Body like syrup on
a stack of pancakes. The poison was sweet and the label
on the bottle read *prosperity*. It would have been so much
easier to grasp the truth, if we had not been indoctrinated
with the *Lie* first. Nevertheless, we are here and the voice
of the Chief Shepherd is about to be heard around the
globe. He will speak to His own first, and then to all who
desire Him.

## THE TRANSFORMATION

As theologians, it is important that we are careful to keep all
script within the context in which they were written. To do
otherwise is a reckless endangerment to the spiritual well-
being of the Body. The doctrine of perfection through the
life of Christ is founded on the revelation of the mystery

that was hidden in God, but is now being revealed to His apostles and latter-day prophets.

Right here I must remind you of the criteria for this study. You must believe on Him the way the scripture has said. Belief is an action word and the action in believing God is to agree. You must agree with that which you learn to be the truth. **There can be no spiritual growth or liberation from mental torment without agreement with God**. In fact, if you do not agree with God's purpose and His methods of obtaining that purpose, then you will surely perish. **The solution to all your problems is to agree with God.** Agree with what God has to say about any subject, and I guarantee you will experience the righteousness, joy and peace that comes with living in the Kingdom.

To *transform* means **to change or make different**. In our case it is for us to become a peculiar people, conformed to the image of the Lord Jesus Christ. *For we ourselves also were sometimes foolish, disobedient, deceived, serving divers lusts and pleasures, living in malice and envy, hateful, and hating one another. But after that the kindness and love of God our Saviour toward man appeared, Not by works of righteousness which we have done, but according to his mercy he saved us, <u>by the washing of regeneration, and renewing of the Holy Ghost</u> (Titus 3:3-5).*

Can it get any plainer than this? We were once disobedient, deceived by sin and served pleasures. However, the new birth changed our spiritual disposition. The issue is how that change was effected.

In the washing of regeneration, there was a sanctification of the body, soul and spirit and a renewing by the Holy Ghost. Therefore, it is possible for you to be perfect in character; not fashioned like the world, but transformed, changed or made different, by the renewing or influence of the Holy Ghost. That is the only way you can live here on earth among a sinful generation but yet prove what is the good, acceptable and perfect will of God (*Rom 12:2*).

**The soul is the spirit of the mind, the heart, the inner man and the spirit of the flesh.** Our soul lives in the Holy Ghost who lives within us. His influence is shed abroad in our hearts (*Rom 5:5*). You now have the mind of Christ. This is the renewing of your mind. God did it. He gave you the mind of the Holy Ghost. He knows that which is acceptable unto God and will never compromise or become deficient.

**Finally beloved, "If we live in the Spirit, then we ought to also walk in the Spirit."** This is the charge given in *Gal. 5:24-25*. In Christ (the Holy Ghost), we live, move and have our being. I submit to you that it is impossible to walk in the Spirit and not have the emotions, desires and purpose of the Spirit. Therefore, any feelings other than that of the Holy Ghost are simply manifestations that you are walking in the flesh. Moreover, please let us not complicate this matter by making it seem like some great mysterious thing to actually walk in the Spirit. To do so is to simply agree with God. If you indeed agree with Him, then you will obey Him. It is as simple as that. Obedience to God is perfection. Obedience to God is a walk in the Spirit.

**I am a witness that agreement and obedience take the struggle out of living holy.** However, take note here that I said agreement and obedience. This is an important point; for it is possible to obey God without being in agreement with Him. Scripture addresses this issue.

**Romans 6:17**
*But God be thanked, that ye were the servants of sin, but ye have obeyed from the heart that form of doctrine which was delivered you.*

Obedience to God must be an act of submission of the heart. It must be without controversy or torment of the soul. There can be no transformation from the way of the world except there is agreement with God. Therefore, if you are experiencing unlawful desires, or emotions that gender ungodly character, then it is evident that you do not agree with what the Word has said about any and every issue. If this is the case, you will never please the Father and you will end up a castaway.

Remember you are a free moral agent now. You are able to choose to obey or disobey the Father and His Christ. It is not hard to obey when you agree with what He speaks in His Word and stand ready to submit to do whatever He wants to do through your body.

I love you very much and I know you will feel the liberty of the Spirit, if you take heed to the counsel of this book. You will be a winner in the battle for the mind; for it is with the mind we serve the Lord. I guarantee you will win the 'Thought War.'

# OTHER MATERIALS FROM
# MARY BANKS FAITH LIBRARY

## STUDY GUIDES

Entering Into God's Rest
From Crack to Christ
The Mystery of Iniquity
The Truth About Women in the Ministry

## STUDY GUIDES WITH CD AND DVD ACCOMPANIMENTS

Amazing Grace
Faith is the Holy Ghost 1 & 2
From the Spirit
How to Study the Bible 1
Journey to the Spirit: Pilgrims passing through
Journey to the Spirit: The Fullness of Christ
Leaders of the Reformation
Lord, Teach Us To Pray
Making of a Minister
Overcoming Emotions and Offenses
Prophetic Voice 1 & 2
The Cost of the Field
The Gift is Holy 1
The Mystery of Christ Revealed
The Power to Mature
Tradition Meets Truth
Volume of the Book 1 & 2
Women of the Reformation

For a more detailed description and additional Study Guides by Mary
Banks, please visit us online at: www.marybanks.net